The Working Homemaker

The Working Homemaker

*Employed Christian Moms
Desiring a Thriving Homelife*

CHARITY GIBSON

WIPF & STOCK · Eugene, Oregon

THE WORKING HOMEMAKER
Employed Christian Moms Desiring a Thriving Homelife

Copyright © 2024 Charity Gibson. All rights reserved. Except for brief quotations in critical publications or reviews, no part of this book may be reproduced in any manner without prior written permission from the publisher. Write: Permissions, Wipf and Stock Publishers, 199 W. 8th Ave., Suite 3, Eugene, OR 97401.

Wipf & Stock
An Imprint of Wipf and Stock Publishers
199 W. 8th Ave., Suite 3
Eugene, OR 97401

www.wipfandstock.com

Biblical quotations are taken from Holy Bible, New International Version®, NIV.® Copyright © 1973, 1978, 1984, 2011 by Biblica, Inc.™ Used by permission. All rights reserved worldwide.

PAPERBACK ISBN: 979-8-3852-2669-6
HARDCOVER ISBN: 979-8-3852-2670-2
EBOOK ISBN: 979-8-3852-2671-9

01/08/25

If you want to change the world, go home and love your family.
—Mother Teresa

Contents

Acknowledgments | ix

Introduction | xi

1. Figuring Out Your Perspective Regarding Your Role as a Working Mom | 1
2. You Can't Have It All or Be It All | 15
3. Let Him Parent, Not Just Play and Provide | 33
4. Less Is More | 49
5. Building Strong Bonds | 69
6. Embracing the Role of Teacher in Our Children's Lives | 87
7. Balancing the Extraordinary Moments with the Ordinary Ones | 106
8. Homemaking that Includes Extended Family | 124

Conclusion | 140

Bibliography | 149

Acknowledgments

I AM SO GRATEFUL to my husband, Ben, and the way that our partnership in our marriage enables me to be a working homemaker who finds joy in the journey. He may not be happy that I do most of my writing at our kitchen counter, but he is nothing but supportive of my writing and my teaching career. He leads and protects our family so well.

I am forever changed by the experience of being a mama and am humbled by the gift of mothering my four children. Without them and what I've learned through having children, I would never have written this book.

I am blessed to have grown up in a home and in a family where homemaking was cultivated, which helped me learn its value and seek to create it in my own home. I'm so thankful for my mom and dad (Marilyn and Larry Higgins) and their example as well as the way they've always believed in my writing.

I am thankful to my talented sister, Cherish Petry, for all her creativity in designing the book cover and taking my picture for the headshot. Her eye for beauty and the sacrificial use of her giftings are a token of love to me.

I am also thankful to Wipf and Stock for taking a chance on an unknown writer with a dream. I'd especially like to thank my editor, Matt Wimer, for his patience in answering my extensive questions and guiding me through this process.

Introduction

I ONCE HEARD IT said that you shouldn't trust an author who has written a book offering advice unless he or she is at least forty years old. The older I get, the more stock I put in the wisdom of lived experience. At thirty-nine, I'm almost at a proposed "age of credibility," according to some standards. Yet there is still a part of me that wonders if I should wait to write this book until I am more seasoned. Maybe I should wait until my kids are out of the house and I can reflect upon raising them. Yet again, by that point, some things won't be fresh. Today I wiped tears, kissed boo-boos, and danced with my five-year-old to a musical rendition of a song created by squeezing a rubber chicken. I'm in the trenches . . . where you likely are too. And that's why I've written this now. Because it's real and raw and beautiful.

Writing a book about parenting, specifically about motherhood, is both a great joy and dream come true and something I doubt I will ever feel qualified to do. There will always be other mothers out there who have more experience, more children, and a better sense of humor in the midst of it all. The market is quite inundated with parenting books. This may not sound like a great way to convince you to read my contribution, but I'll get to that. I'm a Bible-believing, working wife and mom, and I've found that there are not many resources out there specifically focusing on a huge passion of mine: how to apply sound biblical principles to a dual-income family dynamic. There are plenty of books about Christian motherhood or working moms, but not a lot that combine them. Part of my motivation in writing this book has been to write the sort of book that the me ten years ago would have found helpful.

As 71 percent of moms with children at home are in the workforce, balancing work and homelife is far from a new topic. However, I have

INTRODUCTION

only been able to find two books about motherhood in which the title identifies the writers as working mothers who are believers. Of course, there are plenty of logistical reasons for so few, such as time constraints. Yet the lack of books written about Christian working moms' experiences is somewhat surprising since well over half of mothers, secular and Christian, work outside the home. Plenty of books written about Christian motherhood are being written about and read by working women. Yet, the distinctiveness of working outside the home almost appears to have been strategically avoided, instead focusing on the greater shared similarities. And in the end, what unites us is most important.

However, the lack of books about Christian working moms' experience highlights the belief that the art of homemaking and child-rearing best connects with stay-at-home maternal values, while reflections about public life and balancing a busy life connects with working mother values. The myth of the "mommy wars," pitting working moms and stay-at-home moms against each other, has been mostly debunked, but the self-help and betterment genre often suggests that certain values are best held by distinctive lifestyle choices.

This divide is fanned by some who go beyond celebrating stay-at-home mothers to criticizing mothers who make different choices. For example, a well-known Christian organization asserts, "There's a difference between *wanting* to work outside the home and *having* to," suggesting that working mothers are only justified if they have no other alternative but to work. A writer who identifies as a Christian woman on her social media account argues that it is only acceptable for a Christian woman to work if her husband is lazy and forces her do to so, her husband has left the marriage and she must provide for her children, or her husband has died. While such viewpoints are not the norm, they may shed some light on why so few books have been written not just about Christian motherhood but specifically about the nuances of being a Christian mother who works outside the home. Even today, it's a debated topic. It's less controversial to write a book on what connects women, such as Christian motherhood, than to highlight a nuance within it, such as Christian working motherhood, which some disapprove of.

INTRODUCTION

I often feel like I'm teetering between two worlds: the one in which I'm a simplicity-loving mama of four who makes her own elderberry syrup and rarely wears makeup in the summer or Saturdays, and the other in which I'm an English professor with a demanding job and career goals . . . and a couple more kids than most female academics (or the national average). Yes, I admit it—I have a PhD in the humanities. I feel a bit like one of Flannery O'Connor's short story characters, Hulga, who reveals, "I have a number of degrees."[1] But please don't write me off just yet. This is not an academic text, and I'm not planning on lecturing.

I wrote this book specifically for working Christian moms. To be honest, I originally tried to write a book about motherhood in general but didn't get very far because it was hard to talk about motherhood as if all women do it the same way rather than acknowledging my own experiences. I've been a working mama since my children were born. I had four babies in six years and worked throughout all the pregnancies and the child-rearing that came along afterward. Though some of my life choices are different than that of moms who do not work, I believe our end goals for our children are largely the same, so this book is certainly not meant to exclude anyone. But much of it does center on recognizing the dynamics of working and parenting. This book may also be perfect for a mom who is considering working as well as a woman who is not yet a mom but is curious about what being a working mama could look like.

Many resources about working mothers come with images of hurried women juggling a laptop in one hand and a diapered baby (or baby related items) in the other. They talk about how to prep freezer meals and pump at work. And while all those logistics matter, they don't get to the heart of things. I've found that my heart's desires for my family often align closely with my stay-at-home and homeschooling friends who prioritize homemaking. Early on, part of my anxiety regarding working centered around worrying that I would have to sacrifice those fundamental values: prioritizing simplicity, quality and quantity time, and incorporating life-giving family rhythms and rituals because I work. I would like to clarify that none of the stay-at-home moms in my life ever judged me or made me feel inadequate. In fact, several precious stay-at-home moms made it possible for me to work when I had little

---

1. O'Connor, "Good Country People," 446.

ones, partnering with me by watching my baby, and I am forever grateful. My struggle came from what I had internalized regarding myths of bad mothers. However, what I have discovered is that the characteristics commonly valued by stay-at-home moms, though more commonly celebrated in certain family structures, can exist in a variety of family structures. I get asked fairly often by strangers and acquaintances who do not know the ins and outs of our family's situation if we homeschool. I take this as a compliment because I think it means they see certain qualities in our family that are often prioritized by families where the mom stays home. Homeschooling is an intentional lifestyle that requires a degree of distancing oneself from what is typical. Homeschooling culture typically values purposeful parenting and a close-knit family. (I'm speaking from the experience of someone who was homeschooled for eleven years.) However, I have found as a working mom that practicing simplicity, togetherness, and intentionality can happen in a variety of family structures if we are purposeful and willing to be different.

Mother guilt and imposter syndrome are not specific to working women. All mothers question themselves. We all want the best for our children but wonder if what we are giving them is what is right for them. Stay-at-home mothers face the challenge of keeping an identity outside of their role as caregiver. They may encounter the challenge of entering or reentering the workforce once their children are older or grown. They may navigate the constraints of a smaller family budget. They face the criticism of radical feminists who argue they are throwing away their abilities by submitting to patriarchal structures. I do not believe that stay-at-home moms are in any way wasting their time or that they are inferior to working moms. They are faithful laborers in their family and community, and they need resources that speak to their experiences and challenges. However, the same is true for working mothers. We don't love our children less because we aren't with them all day, and we aren't disobeying the Bible. But working Christian mothers also need resources that are specific to our situation, not because it is better or worse than other situations, but simply because it is different.

A fundamental resource difference between stay-at-home moms and working moms is time. Of course, we all have only twenty-four hours in a day, but working mothers spend less time with their children.

INTRODUCTION

This is just math. This book is not about how to rock it at work and keep all the plates spinning at home. This book is not about how to have it all. Supermom and superwoman do not exist. We can have both worlds and maybe even the best parts, but not all parts. It involves sacrifices, compromises, and reevaluated priorities. The premise of this book is acknowledging a limited resource: time. In some ways, this is also not unique to working moms. We all know we get about eighteen years (give or take) with our children before they venture out. However, my focus in this book is how to talk about household practices and dynamics that have specific implications when we recognize the limited amount of time we have to spend with our children. The goal should not be guilt but good stewardship through being purposeful with our greatest resource, time, while also recognizing its finiteness.

The Old Testament describes Jesus and the redemptive work he would come to do as including family restoration: "He will turn the hearts of the parents to their children, and the hearts of the children to their parents" (Malachi 4:6). In the New Testament, John the Baptist is described as the one preparing people's hearts for Jesus, and again it says that this includes a movement "to turn the hearts of the parents to their children" (Luke 1:17). I find it striking that two places in Scripture highlight the importance of living a life submissive to God as a life, for those of us who have children, in which our hearts are turned toward our children. It can be so easy to just go through the motions: to go to work, make dinner, and make sure the kids bathe and do their homework. It can be so easy to live a life based upon what our culture had deemed as normal or good enough to get by. But living a life in which our hearts are turned toward our children is carefully considering how the way we structure our lives leads to their flourishing. This turning of our hearts toward our children does not mean giving them worldly success or a charmed childhood. This turning is "to make ready a people prepared for the Lord" (Luke 1:17). As working moms, we have responsibilities beyond our homes, but part of the kingdom work Jesus came to establish is to call parents who care for their children's spiritual well-being. This does not just mean taking them to church. This includes guiding them in creating healthy boundaries regarding their time and their affections. This includes guiding them in cultivating strong relationships and life lessons. Parents whose hearts are turned toward their children are parents who are homemakers, for the home is where such lessons are cultivated.

We need to redefine the word *homemaker*. Both society and most dictionaries define it similarly to the *Cambridge Dictionary*: "Someone who manages a home and family instead of earning money from employment."[2] Though I recognize the sacrifice stay-at-home moms make, this distinction of viewing working outside the home as separate from nurturing a home and family can be harmful and hurtful to working moms. I propose that a homemaker is any person who values and prioritizes being home and making home a loving and enjoyable place to be, regardless of whether that person also works outside of the home. Sometimes homemaking is misinterpreted as being about interior decorating or gourmet cooking, and some homemakers do have the gift of hospitality and manage a home that is artful as well as inviting. But I am talking about homemaking as a priority rather than a gifting for aesthetics. Homemaking should be something that unites us as women and mothers. I begin with the premise that mothers of all sorts can value being countercultural and desire to incorporate healthy, wholesome rhythms into our homes. I love the way the authors of *Theology of Home II* put it: "Those of us who work also care about making a house a home . . . Ultimately, homemaking is a kind of mothering. Despite what the culture may tell us, all women—despite our vocation—have been hardwired for a kind of fruitfulness."[3] While homemaking certainly entails the physical space of our home, I am extending the definition. The saying "home is where the heart is" relates. Homemaking is not just what we do at home but also the choices we make regarding being away from home that allow for our time at home to be life-giving. Jamie Erickson, the author of *Holy Hygee*, also agrees that homemaking is less about occupation (or lack thereof) and more about heart orientation: "If you're a Christ follower, you're also a homemaker. Your heart is Christ's home, and He's called you to lead others to that same land of promise."[4]

---

2. *Cambridge Academic Content Dictionary*, "homemaker," cited at https://dictionary.cambridge.org/dictionary/english/homemaker.

3. Gress and Mering, *Theology of Home II*, 14.

4. Erickson, *Holy Hygee*, 22.

INTRODUCTION

Apparently, homemaking is making a comeback. There are those who call themselves *radical homemakers* and use the word synonymously with homesteading—living off the land and being self-sufficient from government and commercialization. There are also those embracing what some call the *new domesticity*,[5] which resonates with cool moms who do things like buy and sell from Etsy, post their food creations on social media, and choose wooden, non-battery-operated toys for their children. I readily admit I am far from a hipster homemaker/housewife. I'm not writing about homesteading or the new domesticity. Don't get me wrong—I'm all for making environmentally friendly decisions and finding ways to express ourselves through our motherhood. I believe it's important to celebrate femininity and the work of our hands. The nostalgia of homemaking is somewhat popular right now, highlighting all the things we can patiently produce, such as free-range eggs and knitted cardigans. However, I'm not writing about what's trendy; I'm not cool enough for that anyway. I'm writing about homemaking for what we can cultivate in people rather than produce in goods.

This book is about how to pursue the peaceful rhythms and simplicity of homemaking amidst the dynamics of a dual-income family. I grew up experiencing firsthand the slowed pace that a purposeful lifestyle can offer. But I've also learned that many of the practices of homemaking are not exclusive to teaching from home or refraining from working outside of the home. Furthermore, being home does not necessarily ensure that days are purposeful, that connections with kids are made, and that countercultural practices are implemented. Homes can be toxic and foster dysfunctional relationships. Homes are not automatically warm and inviting places; it takes resolution to cultivate an appreciation for domesticity and a resistance against all the things that can orient our hearts away from home and family. Homemaking is about creating a space where human flourishing can happen. The Lord has said, "My people will live in peaceful dwelling places, in secure homes, in undisturbed places of rest" (Isaiah 32:18). This book is about some of the ways I've learned and continue to strive to take ownership of and cultivate excellence in my role as a Christian working mom. Susan DiMickele insists, "And it's going to take more of us who

---

5. See Matchar, *Homeward Bound: Why Women Are Embracing the New Domesticity*.

INTRODUCTION

are working mothers—mothers who have celebrated success but have learned from failures—to share our experiences with other women and encourage each other as we grow and learn together. Working mothers have much to learn from the church. And yes, the church still has much to learn from working mothers."[6] So, this is my modest addition to the conversation about motherhood, work, homemaking, faith, and the ways they all coincide.

The first few chapters in this book are about understanding why we, as working mamas, have chosen to work and how to navigate our dual roles with a clear vision. The remaining chapters, the bulk of the book, is about doing motherhood small and intentionally as unto the Lord. I am honored that you have picked up this book. Despite all your responsibilities, thinking about how to steward your home will never be a waste of time because society and families will never outgrow the need for homemakers. A wise woman noted, "When we lose the home-makers in a society, we create an emotional homelessness much like street homelessness, with similar problems."[7] I am a fellow traveler on this journey of motherhood along with you and feel so blessed to have the opportunity to share some of the things I have learned. What a privilege it is to be a homemaker.

---

6. DiMickele, *Chasing Superwoman*, 107.
7. "Everyday Heirlooms," 2.

1

Figuring Out Your Perspective Regarding Your Role as a Working Mom

> "You can be a good mom and a working mom.
> You are allowed to be both."
> — ANONYMOUS

THE TERM *WORKING MOM* has some problems. First, it suggests that a working mom, well, works, and a non-employed mom stays home and eats bonbons. All mamas work—some inside the home and some both inside and outside of the home. Furthermore, a distinction between working and stay-at-home moms overlooks all sorts of nuances. Many women occupy both roles or oscillate between them throughout their lives. Women work, take time off, and rejoin the workforce either before and after the years of raising children or intermittently throughout it. Women work part-time. Some technically never leave the home but work remotely while also caring for their children. Now that I've gotten past the obligatory English professor analysis of semantics, let's move on to the ideas people may have about working moms and where those come from.

Because women of the past were expected to marry and bear children, there are some who insist women should be grateful for, and take advantage of, the opportunity to be educated and have a career. Of course, the hypocrisy of swinging the pendulum from "you *must* stay home" to "you *must not* stay home" is not lost. In her famous (and controversial) book *The Feminine Mystique*, Betty Friedan argued that housewives suffered from a "problem that has no name," being that they tired of housework and mothering and wanted an education and career for themselves outside of the home. Friedan is often criticized for devaluing homemaking and, to an extent, she did. However, she is also misconstrued as someone who did not see the roles as mother and worker as compatible. Here is a little of what Friedan actually said: "She [a mother] does not have to choose between marriage and career; that was the mistaken choice of the feminine mystique. In actual fact, it is not as difficult as the feminine mystique implies, to combine marriage and motherhood and even the kind of lifelong personal purpose that once was called 'career.' It merely takes a new life plan."[1] However, the ease with which Friedan suggested women could combine motherhood with work outside the home turned out to be more complicated than she realized. Furthermore, Friedan looked for an earthly solution to a spiritual problem. Women can be dissatisfied with staying home or with working. Changing our circumstances will not change a deep-rooted lack. Friedan looked at stay-at-home mothers' identity as being rooted in their situation; thus, she sought to change their situation to that of a wage-earner to change their identity. However, plenty of mothers are dissatisfied with working as well. Our ultimate identity is neither in the relationships we are involved with nor our earthly accomplishments. Our identity is rooted in Christ and our acceptance of the work he has done for us. We must know who we are because of whose we are. Our purpose is "to glorify God and enjoy him forever."[2]

Although we don't need society's endorsement of our life choices, it is important for working mothers today to know *why* we are working. If you are working because you feel obligated as an empowered woman to do so, let me just remind you of something. You don't owe feminism a career. You don't owe it to other women to carry on the torch. As one woman who left the workforce to care for her children put it, "I've had

---

1. Friedan, *Feminine Mystique*. 468.
2. "Shorter Catechism of the Assembly of Divines."

people tell me that it's women like me that are ruining the workplace because it makes employers suspicious . . . I don't want to take on the mantle of all womanhood and fight a fight for some sister who isn't really my sister because I don't even know her."[3] This sentiment both resonates with me and bothers me. It's true that we should not work just out of principle, to prove that we can or to ensure that someone won't look down on us or other women. Yet this idea that we are all living our own little private lives, that there is no community, no sisterhood, sounds lonely indeed. The truth is you are my sisters in Christ. We must all live our individual lives and travel our own roads, but I do care about your well-being and the struggles all the mamas out there face. There is not a singular vision of what women should be and what they want. We are all created with unique interest, desires, and talents. It's okay that some of us work and some of us don't. It doesn't make any of us more or less of a successful woman or a good mother.

This is a book about the ways in which being a working mama can coincide with homemaking values and fostering a thriving family. But this is not a book that will try to convince you to work if you do not want to work or especially if you feel God is leading you to something else. Women with highly skilled training and education sometimes leave good careers because they want to be home more. And that's okay. Other women stay in or join the workforce. And that's okay too. Maybe you're ambivalent about which kind of woman you want to be. Maybe some days you love your job and other days you just want to stay home to snuggle your littles and maybe catch up on the laundry. In my personal experience, I have learned to trust how I perceive my situation most of the time rather than how I sometimes feel in order to avoid making a significant decision based on temporary emotions.

I have worked full-time during all four of my pregnancies and throughout my motherhood journey. But in the beginning, I agonized over my decision to work. To be honest, I didn't originally anticipate being a working mom, at least not to begin with. Early on, I had dreams of being a college professor but thought that I would probably teach a few adjunct classes as I could during the early years with my babies and then work full-time later. But things went differently than I expected. I

---

3. Belkin, "Opt-Out Revolution."

was blessed with a wonderful teaching job at a small Christian liberal arts college much earlier than I anticipated. By the time I was pregnant with my first, I already had the job I had imagined for myself later in life. To make things even trickier, I was in the very fortunate position in which my institution was financially assisting me through graduate school. If I left, I would have to figure out how to finish paying for grad school without a salary as well as be contractually obligated to repay my institution for everything they had assisted me with up to that point. Or I could quit my PhD program and just be out all the time and money that had already been invested. So, I began motherhood as a working mom because I just didn't feel like it was wise to stop working. I felt I would be letting too many people down if I quit. I enjoyed my graduate studies and teaching. But the guilt I allowed myself to feel about working was heavy.

As I had a degree of job flexibility, I navigated my schedule and responsibilities to do as much of my work as possible from home. I calculated every hour I spent away from my baby and even told people that although I worked full-time, it was really like I worked part-time when I considered how many hours I was away from my daughter. (Of course, I had the full-time work load, but not the on-campus contact outside of teaching and office hours.) It was not that I did not find my work fulfilling or that I did not feel I was making a positive contribution. I lived in the Bible Belt and always had. I had grown up with a stay-at-home mom and had never really experienced the dynamics of a dual-working family. Most of my close friends and family members with children stayed home. Most of my female colleagues were in a different life stage and did not have young children; most of my young male colleagues had wives who stayed home with young children. I didn't feel like I fit in with my close friends who didn't desire to work once they had children, but I also did not fit into the business-woman type who desired to climb the corporate ladder and prove she could break the glass ceiling. I was somewhere in the middle. My roles as a wife and mother were my greatest priorities, but I also felt torn about work. I believed God had gifted me with teaching and writing ability, and part of me wanted to keep working; I was halfway through a PhD program for heaven's sake! But I didn't know exactly how to ensure I could do a good job both at work and home.

Largely to try to make sense of my life and experience, I wrote my dissertation about motherhood, exploring ways that mothers as well as the mother-daughter relationship were portrayed in literature. Reflecting now on the peace that I feel today compared to the angst I often felt then, a few important things have changed. One is that I learned how to stop viewing my situation as something I had to do and started viewing it as a choice I was making. (Disclaimer: I do recognize that I have privilege in choosing whether to work that mothers in poverty do not have. Some mothers must work to make ends meet, and some mothers may want to work but their job will not cover the cost of childcare and thus must stay home.) It can be so easy to talk about work only as a "have to." This is largely connected to social stigmas about working mothers being most acceptable when it is necessary rather than chosen. However, this language of a need versus a want is so subjective. Families have different goals regarding their children's education, activities, and future. What one woman describes as a criteria for her "need" to work will be defined as a "choice" by another. Also, we women have a variety of desires and giftings. Some are material but others are emotional and intellectual. In my experience, though we could have managed financially with some strict budgeting and sacrifices with just my husband Ben's income, all the strings attached to my PhD program made my working feel like a "have to." And that is largely what made me miserable in my miserable moments. (They weren't all miserable.) I would wager that many women think that viewing their work as something they *must* do will alleviate guilt about working, but in my case all it did was take away my agency. I felt I did not get to make that important decision every new mother should be able to make: "Do I want to work or stay home?" (Though again, this does speak to a level of financial security.) Of course, I made the decision ahead of time to enter into a contract that had consequences once I had children, but that didn't change the way I felt.

The thing that really caused me to change my perspective came, as many ultimately good things do, through a very painful and unpleasant set of circumstances. I was prompted to make a choice by my administrator. I remember being called into his office and told I was not going to be allowed to have the same degree of flexibility I had been temporarily granted. I would need to spend more hours on campus. I was told it seemed like I didn't want to be there. When I responded that I did, it simultaneously felt like both the truth and a lie. As I sat there, very pregnant with my third child, sleep deprived, swollen, confused, and angry, I felt torn about whether I was doing the right thing or even able to discern what the right thing was. I tried to make my schedule as flexible as possible but then learned I was not going to be allowed to continue doing that. So, I did what any self-respecting woman would do. I looked for another job as soon as my contractual obligation regarding my funding was about to expire. And I found one . . . I think. I was invited back for a second interview with the president at a different college, so things seemed promising. But I discovered through the interview process that I would not have any more flexibility than I had at my current job. In fact, I might have less. I had to let go of certain illusions about what my work life needed to look like if it was going to be compatible with all the expectations I had placed upon myself to be a good mother. I realized that I was going to have to make a choice. I could leave my job, or I could prioritize motherhood without accepting that meant I must spend all, or even most, of my hours at home. Once I turned down the second interview for the other job and recognized that I was choosing to stay at my current job and accept the expectations rather than the choice being forced upon me, things started to change.

 This is not to say that I never struggle balancing home and work, nor is it to say that I have autonomy regarding all factors of my job. But when we acknowledge that we have made a choice, it allows us to understand why we have made it. It allows us to consider our motivators and our values. When I considered not working, it caused me to deeply consider why I value the things a dual income provides our family: my children's private education, access to good healthcare, life insurance, retirement, and my contribution to society and the common good. Part of my choice was deciding to remain with my current employer. For others, the decision may not be to literally remain at the same job but to choose to work in general. Sometimes there is the element of choice to an extent. For example, perhaps you "have to" work but have chosen the field or the specific job. Sometimes we must make hard choices in some stages to have more ideal circumstances later on. For example, it was hard for me to work while my children were very young because I wanted to be there for all the firsts and to spend a portion of every part of the day with them, which is why I tried so hard to create a flexible schedule early on. However, now that my kids are preschool and school aged, I cannot think of a job with greater flexibility for our family's needs. As an educator, I can spend the summers with my children, as well as holiday breaks. I also work at an institution that values families and offers many activities my family can participate in on campus. It took some patience to get past the early baby years, but I'm so grateful that now our family really benefits from my work culture.

I often hear the word "calling" used regarding both motherhood and employment. This word is often connected with God's perfect will. I absolutely believe that being a mother is one of the most influential things I will ever do on this earth. Besides my relationship with my husband, my relationships with my children are the most intimate relationships I will ever have with other human beings. The level of influence I have over them is vast and humbling. However, when well-meaning people call motherhood a "calling," it discounts several things. First, it ignores the privilege of being a mother, which many women do not have. I don't think God gave me the high calling of being a mother but didn't call other women who have ached for children but have been unable to conceive or who have lost their children. Considering motherhood a calling can inadvertently devalue the role of women who are not mothers. The reality is that for most of us (though I realize not all), motherhood was a choice. We chose to be involved in a relationship that could lead to children, and many of us were either open to or pursued becoming pregnant.

Considering motherhood a calling suggests that it is our primary purpose. This can lead to finding our identity in other people and can create quite a bit of anxiety when our children leave home and our role as primary caregiver changes. Either a career or motherhood can become too revered. Susan DiMickele, a mother of three and trial lawyer, writes, "For working mothers, it's easy to wrap our identity up in our careers, but it's just as easy to wrap our identities into being mothers. Not just any mother, but a *good* mother with obedient—even doting—children."[4] Though our children are more precious than any job will ever be, we must remember that finding fulfillment solely through other people, such as children, still places our value and purpose on something other than God. Our calling in life is to accept Christ's free gift of salvation, consecrate our life to him, and live our daily lives, whatever they entail, for his glory. Ephesians 4:4 clarifies that all believers' calling is much larger than any particular role we hold. "There is one body and one Spirit, just as you were called to one hope when you were called." Our calling is acting upon our hope in Christ. For many of us, motherhood is a big part of our life, but motherhood isn't our actual calling. It can be easy to turn God's story of redeeming the world into an individualized story about us, but the truth is that our story fits into God's bigger story, and not the other way around. First Peter 2:9 notes that our calling is to live a righteous life. "[Y]ou may declare the praises of him who called you out of darkness into his wonderful light." There are a myriad of ways we can live out our calling. When I struggled with whether I should continue working, I was still learning how to prioritize motherhood as an important way I could serve God and others without turning it into an idol by viewing it as my ultimate calling.

Work can also be incorrectly viewed as a calling. This is especially true of helping professions such as teaching. I cannot imagine a career I would have found more fulfilling than teaching. The blessing of working with young people, helping mentor and equip them with skills to communicate with others, has been a great joy. However, teaching is not my calling. I could walk away from my career today and still fulfill God's calling on my life because my calling can be enacted through a variety of situations. God has called us to be good stewards of the talents we have, but we should not mistake an employment opportunity as our purpose. When both motherhood and career are viewed as callings and a person has the mindset that we have only one narrow calling, it can create many a sleepless night regarding which good thing is truly the best thing. I sometimes used to think about my life as a series of closed doors, and I just had to pray hard enough to figure out which "right" door I was supposed to open and walk through while all the other doors

---

4. DiMickele, *Chasing Superwoman*, 215.

stayed closed. What I have learned about God is that when we seek him, he often allows us the gift of choice. As long as we are seeking to honor him, we can choose many of the details of our life. Colossians 3:23 says, "Whatever you do, work at it with all your heart, as working for the Lord." The freedom of "whatever you do" means that we as mamas can equally honor God whether we work or whether we stay home. It's possible that both doors can be open for us. As Edith Stein puts it, "Each woman who lives in the light of eternity can fulfill her vocation, no matter if it is in marriage, in a religious order, or in a worldly profession."[5] Our priorities need to align with biblical principles: our desire should be to love God and to love others. And from there, I have learned to pay attention to my giftings, talents, and preferences.

Now, although neither motherhood nor being an English professor is my ultimate calling, I also must prioritize according to my necessity in those roles. While I strive to be an excellent teacher, I also know that if I left, I would be replaced quickly. In fact, the market is flooded when it comes to thoughtful idealists who believed it would be a good idea to get a graduate degree in the humanities. I have worked with many excellent educators. Students loved them, and they were a joy to work with. But once they retired or resigned, life went on. We were able to hire other competent people, and we all adjusted and moved on. I do not say this to discount anyone's contribution, but I say it for us to humbly acknowledge our own smallness in the grand scheme of things. This is actually a blessing. Nothing depends only on us. God will always raise up new talent, new leaders, new team players in the workforce. My role as my four children's mother is more precious because it is more intimate and more specialized. Jillian Benfield said it well when she wrote, "And then she realized she was replaceable in every area of her life except her home. So she invested her time, her energy, and her heart wisely."[6] Not just any woman can step into my place at home or your place at yours. Yes, technically the cooking, cleaning, and planning can be delegated. But the atmosphere, the example, the influence, the aura we bring to our home is what makes this role so extraordinary. Most women around the world, since the beginning of creation, have been mothers. Yet, each of

---

5. Stein, quoted in Gress and Mering, *Theology of Home II*, 14.
6. Original location of statement unknown.

us mother uniquely and when we do not nurture and guide our home as we have been charged to do, the entire family reels.

Besides embracing my choice to work, the other thing that has brought me peace and confidence about working is seeing the fruit of our family choices. Sometimes when you start something, you step out in faith and wait to see what comes of it. I do not think that a woman should choose to work if her family suffers. Important factors like good childcare, job flexibility, and a threshold for some degree of busyness all influence the outcome. We must be willing to evaluate whether our family structure is working and be willing to change if it isn't. I initially worried that if I was away from my children for portions of the day, we may not bond as we needed to. But my children have never had any confusion about who their mama is, and our bond is stronger than I really imagined possible until I became a parent. I have come to realize that although my children need me every day, they don't need me the entire day. Even if they were home with me, we would spend time apart while they napped and played independently. We have reaped the benefit of having a village in which we have invited other people we trust to pour into our children and positively influence them. Basically, we've seen God bless our family. This is not to say he wouldn't have also blessed us if I stayed home, but it has confirmed for me that God has allowed us the element of choice in seeking a lifestyle that works well for our family.

Both raising a family and working skillfully through labor are ways we can receive God's blessing as we experience joy in these endeavors. In Genesis, God blessed Adam and Eve and encouraged them to be fruitful and multiply, to fill and subdue the earth (Genesis 1:28). God later went on to tell others (Noah and his sons and Jacob) to do the same. The clearest meaning of this instruction is to have families. This exhortation toward fertility celebrates our work as wives and mothers. However, God does not limit the ways in which we are to be fruitful and to fill the earth. Indeed, there are many good things people have been faithful to fill the earth with. Contributions to art, literature, science, music, sports, culinary, business, and the list goes on are other ways that through their labor people have filled the earth with good things. As one theologian puts it, "By growing things and developing culture, we are indeed fruitful . . . The human task is to extend the creative work of God in a multitude of ways."[7] God blesses us by allowing us to be part of the filling of the earth. We fill it through bearing and raising our children, and we fill it through doing meaningful work that blesses others.

If the call to filling the earth only related to procreation, then key biblical figures such as Jesus and the apostle Paul acted against this. Yet we know both Jesus and Paul cultivated fruitful ministries for God's glory. Both families and work can be tainted through improper goals and priorities, but they can also both be offered to God in obedience. Raising our families to be salt and light in the world is a pivotal way we can live a fruitful life. However, it is not the only way, as those who have not had children often attest. Doing good work enriches our lives and those of others. Filling the earth with good things produced by our work can happen from both paid and unpaid labor. A woman who is not employed outside the home still works in ways that can positively impact others. However, it can be useful for those of us who are employed to remind ourselves that our occupations, when viewed as service to the Lord, all allow opportunities for us to be fruitful and multiply. We may be producing a service for others, we may be multiplying knowledge, or something else. Whatever our employment entails, recognizing that it, just like our commitment to our family, can bring fruitfulness can remind us of its value.

So where then did this idea that mothers are forsaking their calling if they work come from? To a degree, it stems from historical revisionism. We have probably all heard that the traditional family structure is one in which the mother stays home with the children. However, some important details regarding what motherhood looked like in the past have been overlooked. While women did stay home, they did not stay home alone, and they did not solely rear the children. The divide between the public sphere (work force) and private sphere (home) that we have today is a product of modernity and the Industrial Revolution. Traditionally, both the husband and wife worked together to farm, garden, homestead, or whatever other trade the family engaged in. They both worked, and they both saw to the rearing of the children. A sociologist explains that before the mid-nineteenth century, frontier women performed a variety of roles on a farm and that "a woman's child-rearing

---

7. Theology of Work Project, "God Creates and Equips."

function was less important for family survival than her farm and household-related money-raising activities."[8] Traditionally, women and men both worked from home, but due to changes in the workforce and most employment being removed from the home, men began leaving to work while women remained at home. Over time, the idea of motherhood being something separate from economically supporting the family emerged. Christian professor of religious studies John Stackhouse Jr. confirms that there are misunderstandings regarding what a traditional family means: "This sort of family is actually not found in the Bible anyway, or in most of the history of the church. The ideal family touted by so many North American evangelical preachers is an artifact of a very particular era: the post-World War II boom in which a man could earn a household's worth of income even on an assembly line."[9] While a family is not in error if they value a family dynamic in which the dad works and the mom stays home, the mistaken idea that this is the superior model because it is traditional overlooks the fact that it only dates back to the Industrial Revolution.

In modern times, poor women also left the home to work, but a wife who did not work became a symbol of social class and "having a wife at home signaled middle-class status."[10] While it is well within women's rights to want to stay home, the idea that a woman staying home to watch the children is the traditional model is inaccurate. As another scholar puts it, the belief that mothers at home focused only on child-rearing and domestic duties "is an historical aberration of twentieth-century industrialized life."[11] In contrast to one woman staying in her own home to care for her children, in tribal or village cultures where women stayed home while men went out to work, hunt, or forage, the women reared the children in communities that included "the very young, very old, unmarried, and infertile women in the process of 'mothering.'"[12] This historical research neither supports nor criticizes a mother's decision to either stay home or work. However, it does suggest

8. Lindsey, *Gender Roles*, 246.
9. Stackhouse, *Partners in Christ*, 118.
10. Williams, *Unbending Gender*, 157.
11. Maushart, *Mask of Motherhood*, xx.
12. Rich, *Of Woman Born*, 12

that both the typical stay-at-home model and the working model for contemporary mothers are drastically different from truly traditional models.

More important than historical models, however, is biblical truth. We should care much less about what people have done than we care about what God says we ought to do. Verses like Titus 2:4–5, which says, "Urge the younger women to love their husbands and children, to be self-controlled and pure, to be busy at home," clearly show the importance of mothers valuing our role as homemakers. While there are some who interpret this verse to mean that mothers should only stay home, the text does not specify this, and many theologians claim that it simply means prioritizing our home and our family. Nothing else we do should prevent us from working to make our home a loving and comfortable place for our family to dwell and grow. The Bible gives us examples of women who managed mothering and working well. Proverbs 31 speaks of a woman who earns an income ("out of her earnings she plants a vineyard," verse 16) and excels in the workplace ("She makes linen garments and sells them, and supplies the merchants with sashes," verse 24). Her family does not just get by; rather, they thrive. "Her children arise and call her blessed; her husband also, and he praises her" (verse 28). This example from Proverbs 31 does not dictate that women must be industrious outside of the home, but it certainly makes a case for the ability of working mothers to also be conscientious and successful homemakers. Lydia, the seller of purple cloth in the New Testament, is another example of a working mother. After she became a believer, she and her entire household were baptized. There are some that use Lydia as an argument for infant baptism, suggesting that she had young children or even babies who were baptized.[13] I'm not using this verse to comment on infant baptism but instead to note that it is often assumed that Lydia's household included children. Lydia is celebrated as a "worshiper of God" and someone of whom "the Lord opened her heart" (Acts 16:14). Both the Proverbs 31 woman and Lydia are examples of working mothers in the Bible who are shown to be living out their calling to glorify God through both their roles as mothers and as paid workers.

---

13. "Infant Baptism."

The Working Homemaker

Being a mama isn't for the faint of heart. No matter the age of the children or the status (working mother or otherwise), it's challenging. But though hard work comes with the territory—the Proverbs 31 woman herself got up before sunrise!—self-doubt and guilt are only hindrances and are not of God. Every woman should be able to make the decision for herself whether to work rather than feeling obligation (though, of course, logistics such as finances play a key role.) If you work and plan to keep doing so, which I'm assuming you do if you picked this up and have read this far, you can find confidence through acknowledging the element of choice in your situation. The romanticized notions about traditional motherhood are often inaccurate. Our goal should not be to align with some mythical idea of what motherhood used to be but instead to have realistic visions of the sort of moms we can, through God's help, actually be. We can, through God's grace, not just survive but thrive in our roles as working moms. We do not have to choose between work and homemaking. Our God-given calling is something larger than our connection to our family or a career, though we should use them both for his glory. However, as I'll go on to explore soon, this does not mean we can have it all either. There are limitations and hard choices to be made, but in my experiences, those boundaries and choices are easier to make and respect when we are passionate about our choices and our goals. So, let's know what we're about, and then go about it.

2

You Can't Have It All or Be It All

"The most important work you'll ever do will be in your own home."[1]
—Harold Lee

WOMEN IN THE WORKPLACE are a force to be reckoned with. Our attention to detail, talent for organization, and ability to connect on a relational level has made the workplace a more humanized and enjoyable place for everyone. A student who works in my building was recently going around to professors' offices, taking out trash for everyone. When she came to me, she shared what she had observed on her tour. The men made their offices look like offices, and the women made our offices look like homes. This testament to womanhood and our desire to bring warmth and comfort not only into our own homes but the workspaces we welcome others into speaks to the way the workplace has benefitted from a feminine presence. However, more women are finding that we may have different goals than many of our male colleagues. The term *gender wage gap* suggests that men and women receive a different salary for doing the same work. The term *glass ceiling*[2] suggests that women are only allowed, due to invisible systemic barriers, to advance so far in their career. These issues have been large obstacles to women of previous

1. Original location of statement unknown.
2. Loden, panel discussion at the Women's Action Alliance.

generations who were paid less than men and denied opportunities for sexist reasons. If men and women are being paid unequally for doing the same job though they have the same amount of experience or if women are being denied opportunities they are qualified for, this is an injustice.

Yet, not all job and salary differences between men and women today are due to injustice. The element of choice, which is something I talked about in chapter 1 in a different context, is again relevant in understanding women's earnings. As one economist puts it, "It's an important, but overlooked point that there really is no gender wage gap, rather, there's a gender earnings gap and that pay gap has almost nothing to do with gender discrimination."[3] Many women choose not to pursue a high-paying or high-status job because it requires more time away from family, and this is a form of sacrifice we should honor women for making. Some argue that there is an *ambition gap*, meaning women are at fault for not being as driven as men. However, John Stackhouse Jr. suggests, "Many women, like some men, refuse to accept a narrow definition of life success that entails leadership in a hypermale mode: maximum individual power, maximum individual prominence, maximum individual compensation, and so on. Many women simply refuse to play this terrible game."[4] When we could do everything in our power to catch our bosses's or others' attention and instead content ourselves with doing our job well and leaving our schedules open so that we have both the physical and emotional energy we need to be there for our family, we are being working homemakers. The American Enterprise Institute notes that men are more likely than women to choose jobs that have higher safety risks or physically demanding environments, require longer hours, require longer commutes or travel, require more financial and emotional risk, require more training and uninterrupted experience, and offer higher pay though less fulfillment.[5] The sacrifices that many women are unwilling to make in the workforce seems to speak to an innate desire we have to remain available for investment in our personal lives, often through relationships, and for moms this largely

3. Perry, "There Really Is No 'Gender Wage Gap.'"
4. Stackhouse, *Partners in Christ*, 163.
5. Perry, "There Really Is No 'Gender Wage Gap.'"

centers on our families. However, such decisions often mean less worldly success than jobs that require more risk and demands.

Some of the reasons that women earn less are based on situational circumstances, like the need to be home with a sick child, be available for appointments, or take time off for maternity leave. The workplace needs to improve so that working moms are not penalized for shouldering these important responsibilities. We need to normalize involved fathers who also take time off to help with family responsibilities. Social norms can also influence jobs women gravitate toward. If girls don't pursue STEM jobs because they have been told girls can't be good at math and science, this is a problem. If women don't pursue management positions because of social stigmas that incorrectly teach that women do not have leadership qualities, this is a problem. However, many of the reasons women choose less-lucrative or prestigious jobs are based on values that impact life choices. We want to spend as much time with our children as we can. I believe this is a God-given desire.

Any time there is a conversation about differences in men and women's actions, there is always a debate over whether this is due to created differences or social influence, basically nature or nurture. Some would argue that women only choose more family friendly jobs because we have been conditioned to believe that we should. I do not discount nurture. Culture certainly enforces ideas about what is traditionally masculine and feminine. Many of these ideas are stereotypical; girls can, in fact, like colors besides pink, and not all boys enjoy football. Not everyone fits into gendered categories, and they should not be forced to. However, as J. Budziszewski notes, although we all have personal preferences that extend beyond gender, all cultures have recognized differences between boys and girls and have raised them accordingly. Budziszewski asks, "[I]f the pattern of upbringing has no basis in human nature, why is it so persistent?"[6] The fact that all cultures have noted women's caregiving tendencies suggests that most women instinctively possess an ability and desire to care for others. This does not mean that caregiving is all that women can do, but it suggests something universal within femininity. When you look at the anatomy of men and women's brains, the differences are just as pronounced, suggesting that differing

---

6. Budziszewski, *On the Meaning of Sex*, ch. 3.

actions, though influenced to an extent by society, are also ingrained due to brain chemistry. According to *Stanford Medical Magazine*, evidence suggests that there are "inherent differences in how men's and women's brains are wired and how they work."[7] Understanding physical differences between men and women not just in obvious sexual ways but in brain construction helps us understand why we gravitate toward certain types of employment.

God gave men the desire to be providers and protectors; this only intensifies once they become husbands and fathers. This connects to the way they were created. Even studies conducted from a non-biblical worldview have noted the inherent differences in men and women's brain chemistry. According to the author of *The Male Brain,* men "have larger brain centers for muscular action and aggression, which relate to protection and defense."[8] God has called men to be providers because he has already given them the desire to do so. First Timothy 5:8 says, "But if any provideth not for his own, and specially for his own household, he hath denied the faith, and is worse than an unbeliever" (ASV). This does not mean mothers do not also want to provide for and protect our children, but women do not typically see it as our duty to provide financially for our families in the same way God has charged men. The verses about biblical headship speak not to a husband's dominance over his wife but his responsibility to be the example and the one to whom ultimate responsibility falls: "[T]he head of every man is Christ, and the head of the woman is man, and the head of Christ is God" (1 Corinthians 11:3). In the Bible, any time a family's safety or survival was threatened, God always spoke to the husband as the protector who should take action (Noah was told to build an ark for his family; Lot was visited by an angel to lead his family out of Sodom; Joseph received a dream to reserve grain in Egypt for the upcoming famine; and Joseph the earthly father of Jesus was told by an angel to take Mary and baby Jesus to Egypt to escape Herod.) Men bond with their children by "helping to solve their problems and fixing things that are broken."[9] Though fathers also must evaluate their priorities and whether their career goals are beneficial for

---

7. Goldman, "Two Minds."
8. Brizendine, *Male Brain*, 4.
9. Brizendine, *Male Brain*, 93.

their families, in my experience and observations, men do not struggle with being away from their children the same way women do because being away allows for men to fulfill their fundamental desire to stabilize and provide. It is for these reasons that men are more likely to gravitate toward jobs that have greater risk, time, and energy requirements.

One of our God-given desires as women is to be nurturers. Studies show that due to brain differences, women show more empathy and compassion than men when we see someone in pain or discomfort.[10] This does not mean that men should not also learn how to nurture or that caregiving comes naturally to all women. But overall, most mothers greatly care about nurturing our families. This is one of the reasons that, if possible, we want to be the one to care for our sick kiddo. Women are created with a great capacity to develop relationships and to bond with those we care about. The Bible talks about women's influence in the home: "The wise woman builds her house, but with her own hands the foolish one tears hers down" (Proverbs 14:1). It also talks about the natural inclination we feel toward our children: "Can a mother forget the baby at her breast and have no compassion on the child she has borne?" (Isaiah 49:15). This is not to say fathers do not also have a pivotal role to play at home, but their brains are wired to prioritize providing over nurturing, whereas women value nurturing even when we also provide. A mother's ability to influence her household for good or harm are presented through a variety of biblical stories. Showing ways women can misdirect, Rebekah's influence over Jacob in guiding him to deceive his father and obtain his brother's birthright comes to mind. The evil queen Jezebel is notorious for her bad influence on her husband, King Ahab, but she also led her three children—all future rulers of Israel and Judah—astray. Contrastingly, many heroes of the faith were carefully nurtured by strong mothers. Jochabed, Moses' mother, and Hannah, Samuel's mother, raised sons whose hearts remained faithful to God their entire lives, despite their leaving home at a young age. Paul noted the influence that mothers have on their children: "I am reminded of your sincere faith, which first lived in your grandmother Lois and in your mother Eunice and, I am persuaded, now lives in you also" (2 Timothy 1:5). All these examples relate to understanding why many

---

10. Brizendine, *Female Brain*, 120–22.

women choose jobs with more flexibility for family. Children who suffer from their mothers working suffer not inherently from being away from their mothers but from the stress some jobs cause. Researchers found that "mothers' negative employment experiences create personal strains. The personal strains, in turn, affect parenting behaviors. Finally, parenting behaviors affect children's behaviors."[11] So, the jobs we hold and the careers we pursue impact our children because they impact us and our availability to parent them well. As working homemakers, we must recognize the role we play in our children's development and the responsibility involved with being a homemaker and choose our outside employment thoughtfully.

Marriage and motherhood are not for everyone, and I would never attempt to persuade a woman who does not desire such things to pursue them. However, many successful businesswomen have had to sacrifice having a family, even if they desired one. A study by the *Harvard Business Review* found that 49 percent of what they call "corporate business achievers" are childless.[12] Part of this may be because the foundation for a successful career is built during a woman's childbearing years. For some women, infertility later in life plays a part, and for other women, their schedules simply do not allow for motherhood. Part of the issue is social expectations about what woman's work entails. If every family-related responsibility falls to women, it makes working outside the home difficult to impossible. However, even women with husbands who share the load, myself included, find that we do not want to delegate all our domestic duties for the sake of career advancement. Managing our homes well grounds us to our families; it roots us in the refining process of habitual work. Homemaking is a form of loving our husbands and children.

Sometimes our ideas of how we can make all the pieces fit if we just have the right attitude are manipulated through well-meaning stories. Movies like *The Intern* with Anne Hathaway highlight the very real challenges that being a successful CEO entails. Jules (Hathaway's character) is overwhelmed and rarely home due to her demanding job. Near the end of the film, Jules discovers her husband, Matt, has been

---

11. Otto et al., "Maternal Employment Experiences," 501.
12. Hewlett, "Executive Women."

cheating on her, and she plans to resign for the sake of her personal life. Yet at the film's end, she and her husband both promise to invest more in their marriage and their young daughter while Jules maintains her demanding job. Messages like this suggest that working wives and mothers can keep all the plates spinning if we just try hard enough. But the unresolved issue in *The Intern* is that nothing changes in the way Jules and Matt conduct their schedules, yet they expect their home life to magically recover.

In a similar way, the movie *I Don't Know How She Does It* stars Sarah Jessica Parker as Kate, a working mom who lives a fast-paced life and works a demanding job. In the climax of the film, the family almost falls apart due to Kate's frequent work trips and her estrangement from her husband, Richard, and their two children. At the end of the film, Kate apologizes for prioritizing her work over her family but seemingly plans to continue at her current job and simply try to show her family more how much she loves them despite her job's constraints.

Both *The Intern* and *I Don't Know How She Does It* highlight a myriad of factors that make employment demanding for mothers. The films also point out how torn working mothers can feel. However, they both ultimately suggest that women can have any job they want, and if they just remember how much they love their family, all will be well. However, this is just not true. Though I fully support mamas in their endeavor to work, society is doing women and families a disservice by pretending that women can have it all. You only have so much water you can pour out of your bucket. If we do not guard our water supply to nurture the seeds we are raising at home, we won't be able to pour into them as they need us to. I daily tell my children I love them, and I'm sure you do too. But I've learned my words are not all they need. My actions need to assure them of the truth of my words. Loving is being there; loving is being able to be present physically and emotionally. It's showing up consistently.

I came across some testimonials of working women in demanding jobs that add some realism to the fictional films I just mentioned. One mother said that her nanny did all the menial tasks like shopping for her son's clothes so that she could spend her limited time interacting with her son rather than doing mundane chores and responsibilities.

Another mother said that because her travel schedule did not allow for her to attend all her children's activities, she had her kids make A, B, and C lists in which they ranked their life events in order of importance. She went to the A-list events and missed the rest. Now, I want to say this carefully because I am not in a place to judge anyone. We are meant to encourage one another, not tear each other down. Mothers who spend more time with their children than I do could have judged me and have not, and I am grateful. But society is selling us, as working women, the lie that we can have it all. If we can just find the right babysitter to help or the perfect planner to prioritize, we can achieve as much as possible at work and still have a thriving family. But that's a lie. Part of the blessing of motherhood is the way we are refined through sacrifice. Being willing to sacrifice our desires or even career potential is not a popular message today. Yet, we are called to sacrifice, and if we have a family, they are our greatest sphere of influence. We can hold roles outside of parenthood, but if those positions require us to nickel-and-dime our time and attention available to our children and husbands, it may be time to reconsider. Quality time is important, but it is not the only thing our children need from us. The quantity of time is also important. We need to be available to hang out together even when there is nothing scheduled.

We don't have to be perfect housekeepers, but when we make good use of our family's resources and ensure that our family is fed and clothed, that is also a form of loving them well. This does not mean we should hesitate to make use of resources that can make things easier. I am all about my subscription for Walmart grocery delivery. Before I started this, I did online ordering and store pick-up. I don't think that scouring the aisles of the grocery store makes me a more engaged mom than ordering online and having groceries delivered. In fact, it gives me more availability to spend with my family. However, there may be other tasks I could outsource that would disengage me from my family, so I have committed to doing them myself. Our family needs our presence, and they also need the organization and structure we provide when we oversee things they don't even notice. This may have been what Solomon was talking about regarding the virtuous woman: "She watches over the activities of her household" (Proverbs 31:27.) When we are sitting on the bleachers at the ball game, even if they barely acknowledge our presence, we are providing our child with the support that they know we are there for them.

It's not about being there for everything. We are going to miss some things, and we must give ourselves grace for that. I can't make fieldtrips that my kids go on during the school day. I travel for conferences a couple times a year and miss the activity that happens that weekend. But our norm is that we spend evenings and weekends together. I do not say this to boast, but I say it to share that prioritizing family and still doing well at work is possible. We are all going to have busy seasons. There are days I have an evening event I go back to campus to attend or facilitate. But that is not what our typical days look like. A quote that is becoming popular (originally by Betty Friedan) regarding women balancing family and careers is, "You can have it all, just not all at the same time." But I don't think this is true. Not all opportunities have an extended shelf life. When we say no to something, sometimes we must acknowledge that it is for good. We can't have it all . . . ever. Some of the most celebrated women writers were childless; Jane Austen, Charlotte and Emily Brontë, Willa Cather, Virginia Woolf, Edith Wharton, Emily Dickinson, and Louisa May Alcott all come to mind. Many have noticed, especially in earlier times, that women achieving success in their careers or craft required a level of devotion and availability that is difficult for mothers to give. This does not mean we cannot have fulfilling careers, but if we value homemaking and prioritize it, we may have to say no to some types of professional success. It's best to acknowledge this so that we are not resentful later if the same sort of career success is not available once our children are older or grown.

I never pursued a tenure-track job where the expectation to regularly publish books or articles in top-tier journals is high. The phrase in my field for those jobs is "publish or perish." It's quite possible I couldn't have landed a tenure-track job anyway; I'll never know. This is not to say no mothers on the tenure track can do it well; I have been blessed to have had several impressive professors mentor me who also maintained family responsibilities. Each woman must decide for herself what her limits are and what prioritizing homemaking means for her and her family. But I know I personally could not be the mother I desire to be with the expectations of a tenure-track job. I am not alone in this, as only 44 percent of tenured women professors have children.[13] Those who do typically have fewer children than I have. Most tenured women professors also have fewer children than their male colleagues. One woman has admitted she thinks they are all a little bit heartbroken about it. While I'm grateful for the contribution these working moms are making, I also wonder if something is amiss if working women feel compelled to give up the number of children they desire in order to achieve career success, doing their best to hide their disappointment in the process. While personal preference, health concerns, fertility issues, and economic situations certainly influence most people's family size, for me, being a working homemaker includes first choosing our family dynamic, such as the number of children we desired, rather than determining our family size based upon the demands of a career. It can be tempting to want to prove the statistics wrong, to be what the odds say we can't be. But there is also humility in looking at others around us and learning from their experience. Not trying for a tenure job or a placement at a graduate school has been a way for me to practice humility and simplicity and resist outward ideas of career success. I believe I have chosen well in working at a like-minded college that prioritizes professors who love teaching and appreciate a schedule that allows for family flourishing.

Yet, even at my institution, I have still made decisions that have, to a degree, impacted my career. I guard my summers and do not teach grading-intensive classes that are outside of my contractual duties while my children are off during the summer months. I am not pursuing becoming a director, chair, or administrator. Some women may hold these roles and manage well, and some stages of life and motherhood may be better for such undertakings, but at this stage in my life, I believe this would overextend me. And I am very much at peace with my role at work. I have been promoted to an associate professor and will soon be eligible to be become a full professor. I am not suggesting that we should be poor workers. We should do our work to honor God in a way that is above reproach. We should respect our employers or business (for those who are self-employed) and bless those we serve. I love being a professor

---

13. Mason, *Do Babies Matter?*

and work hard to be a good teacher and an involved faculty member on campus. However, the American Dream model suggests that there is always something more to strive for: the next tier, the next pay bump. The workplace is not designed to celebrate people who complete the job description. It valorizes productivity by celebrating going above and beyond. However, there are only so many areas of our life in which we can go above and beyond. It just comes down to math.

When I started researching for this project, I found plenty of books about being a working mom, mostly from secular perspectives. The covers of these books typically showed a harried woman in heels juggling diapers and a briefcase. Book jackets showed frazzled women, despite outward signs of success such as sporting fashionable clothes and trendy technology. One showed a mom pulling lagging children along behind her, while another showed a mom holding a child in her lap while she distractedly works on a computer. These images ignited something in me. I felt compassion for these women but also felt frustrated that this lifestyle has been normalized as good enough or just what inevitably happens if a mom works. Abbie Halberstadt writes about not justifying mediocre motherhood just because it is becoming socially acceptable. She says that "we may discover that we fit in just fine and can always manage to find someone to justify our shortcomings or make us feel better about our bad days. But we will not have found, at the end of it all, that we look much like Jesus or that we have gotten any closer to feeling at peace with motherhood."[14] A flourishing career may be an excuse for a hectic family life, but our goal should not be a life we can justify but a life we can offer as a pleasing sacrifice to God. He is more interested in our faithfulness to the people he has given us than our striving to achieve more. We should give ourselves grace to be imperfect moms but not allow that to become an excuse for parenting our children just well enough to get by.

We can pursue a life that allows for us to mother with energy and vision. This does not mean things won't be messy and we will never grow weary, but being working homemakers requires marathon vision rather than sprint vision to just make it through the day or to the weekend. Our employment needs to complement our ability to mother our families well

---

14 Halberstadt, *M Is for Mama*, 18.

for the long haul. My desire as a working homemaker is to hold myself to a high standard at work and to hold myself to an even higher standard at home. This doesn't mean I'm being supermom. It's only possible through selecting outside employment that allows for some margin to protect homelife as well as embracing simplicity over busyness at home. Despite my love of coffee, I have recognized that ample caffeine (working mothers on the front cover of books are usually pictured with coffee) will not be enough to keep all the plates spinning. Actually, I don't just want to keep the plates spinning. I want to set them down on the table and invite my family in together to eat something nourishing and warm together, even if it has to be reheated. The only way work and family can mesh well is by creating boundaries, acknowledging limitations, and embracing sacrifice as a form of love.

The *mommy track*[15] is a term for working women who, due to their mothering responsibilities, have different career trajectories than men or childless working women. Typically, this is a dirty word that points out ways women are stifled. If a woman wants to pursue career advancement, shows her capability for doing so, and is denied because her employer anticipates she will not be successful because of her responsibilities at home, this is an injustice. However, I would like to redeem the term *mommy track*. I am okay hedging my ability for career success within the parameters of what is healthy for my family. And though the mommy track influences our entire lives, the years in which we intensively raise our families are not a permanent situation. As it says in Ecclesiastes, "There is a time for everything, and a season for every activity under the heavens" (3:1). I have worked with various women, and observed others, who were on the mommy track for years, slowing down or taking a break from work entirely to raise their children, who rejoined the workforce later. I wouldn't say they eventually had it all. They made sacrifices that impacted their careers. Yet, I have seen them flourish at work, the wisdom of their years of mothering serving as an asset. Life is long, and even though we should be honest with ourselves about what is worth sacrificing for our families and what that could mean professionally, there are also beautiful stories of mothers whose careers bloomed later. Laura Ingalls Wilder didn't publish her first book

---

15. Kingson, "Women in the Law Say Path is Limited by 'Mommy Track.'"

until she was sixty-five years old. Toni Morrison published her Pulitzer Prize–winning novel when she was fifty-six.

The criteria for what is healthy for a strong family culture will look a little different for each family, and there is freedom in that. Our own desires, personalities, threshold for busyness, and the needs of our husbands and children all factor in. For me, being able to drop off my kids at school most days is important. Having a job with summer flexibility is important. Having a job that doesn't keep me from attending church with my family on Sunday mornings is a necessity. Your work and schedule may look different than mine, and I am not proposing a one-size fits-all approach—that would be legalism. However, acknowledging the need for a flexible schedule is something more women have begun to insist upon. And in many jobs, it is something that has benefits for everyone. The ability to work from home largely influences things, as the pandemic highlighted. A 2023 survey conducted by the International Workplace Group found that 88 percent of respondents believed hybrid working models help equalize the workplace. Seventy-two percent of women said they would look for a new job if they could no longer have a hybrid work schedule.[16] Sometimes we think it is unreasonable to want job flexibility, but more working mamas are recognizing its benefits and standing up for themselves in requesting it.

Although research has begun showing reasons to update rigid 8–5 workday schedules,[17] some of us have been hurt by insinuations that we are not hard workers because we have boundaries regarding how much we will allow our jobs to impact our homelife. This is hard to swallow when we are working so hard both at home and at work. Please know that you are not alone. And please know that God sees. He sees the hours you are putting in at work. He sees the hours you are putting in to serve your family. You are not lazy because you do not desire to climb to the highest rung on the career ladder. And even with flexibility and hybridity, it will never make being a working homemaker easy. But hard doesn't mean bad. We can do hard things. We just have to make sure that the things we are working so hard for are really the things we want and are really the things that matter.

16. McKendrick, "Another Benefit of Hybrid Work."
17. Zucker, "Breaking Free from a 9–5 Culture."

The Working Homemaker

For many working moms, flexibility is something that can be helpful and that is worth pursuing. However, a con of working from home is that it blurs the line between home and work. It can be difficult enough to mentally switch gears, but when home also serves as a workspace for paid employment, as well as all the domestic work we do there, it can lead to our never resting. To avoid working overtime at the office, I do bring work home. I have found that giving myself a schedule, such as grading and lesson prepping on weeknights but not usually on the weekends, which I reserve for family time and household chores, helps me.

While some jobs better allow for home/work balance than others, there are many different schedules and careers where we can find purpose and fulfillment, and this diversity is something to celebrate. I have found that some of the skills I have cultivated as a homemaker are the unique talents I bring to my department. Planning fun and interactive activities is something I do often for my children; I value giving them experiences, and I do the same thing for my college students. I'm known in my department for being someone to organize fieldtrips and game/movie nights as well as more formal events like conferences and banquets. Some of the organizational skills that I have honed raising four children also helps me in organizational tasks at work such as creating the semester schedule, managing the budget, or organizing the writing contest. The care I daily practice toward my family is also something I try to use to minister to my students. One student recently described me as a "motherly teacher." Another told me I reminded him of his mom and thought we would get along, which, aside from the fact I'm not old enough to be his mother unless I'd had him extremely young, I took as a compliment. In using our strengths as mothers at work, we can be examples not just for our own daughters but for other people's daughters. I am very aware that my students who are young women are thinking about their future and wondering what it can look like. Psychiatrist Anna Fels calls the modeling more experienced women can offer younger ones an *imagined future*.[18] Though I do not suggest to any of my female students that they need to work, I am humbled when they let me know that maybe I have played a very small part in helping them see themselves as a working mama someday. These are a couple

---

18. Fels, *Necessary Dreams*.

encouragements I have received from students: "Thank you for showing me that I can be a mom and a professor—your influence gives me hope and a model for my life." "I look up to you very much as you are a wife, mom, and awesome professor (my dream life some day)."

First of all, please know that these notes are not a regular occurrence. In fact, every semester after reading course evaluations, there are also some comments that are so less than kind I run straight to the ice cream and chocolate. But I include these snippets from notes to encourage you that someone is watching. You don't have to do it perfectly to show them it's possible. One year I found this in a course evaluation: "Dr. Gibson is literally my hero. She utilized the virtual learning tool multiple times as she was in quarantine. There was even a time when her son would not go to sleep and she taught class with him in her lap. This was not a hindrance whatsoever and she taught class with professionalism." Clearly, teaching and holding my son does not qualify me as a hero, but this comment shows how separate the family and the workspace often are in most people's minds. This was shortly after the height of the pandemic, and anytime a daycare teacher had COVID, my son's entire class was quarantined for two weeks, so I spent a fair amount of time teaching virtually from home. It was not ideal. But it was real life for a parent, and my students got to see that. When a student a few years ago wrote me on a Sunday in May to wish me a Happy Mother's Day, I almost cried. The fact that she saw me not just as her professor but as a mother and celebrated me for both is all I could ask for. This is not to say I get everyone's stamp of approval. I have had a student in a course evaluation write that I have too much on my plate and should be spending more time at home with my young family. And this student, whom I would bet money is a young lady, is entitled to her opinion. I've learned I don't need everyone's validation that I'm living my life as I should. I am at peace; I have witnessed the Lord's goodness at home and at work, and it is enough.

Being a literature professor has also helped me understand my roles through the ways I see them mirrored or altered in the literature I teach. There may be a misconception that only men feel the need to accomplish something. I teach an American drama class, and one of the central themes that occurs time and again in one play after another is the men's desire to achieve financial security and public success. Contrastingly, the women long for a stable home and family life. I find myself caught in the middle. I absolutely resonate with the women and the innate desire we usually feel to care for our families and provide a nurturing place to do life together. However, this doesn't mean I don't also want to make a place for myself in the world. I want people to know I am capable, intelligent, and able to keep up. In Arthur Miller's famous play *Death of a Salesman*, Willy Loman, an aging traveling salesman, incorrectly thinks that to have a successful life, he must lead a big life. "Very big" is his common description of anything worthwhile.[19] He exaggerates his own popularity and salary to impress others and does the same regarding his sons once they are grown. The play reminds me that it is normal to want to achieve some sort of quantifiable success for others to notice. Ultimately, though, Willy's relationship with his wife and sons deteriorates because he has prioritized appearance over authentic relationships. Though Linda, Willy's 1950s housewife, appears immune to the need to prove her worth, this may be an oversight on Miller's part. Women, just like men, feel the need to not only nurture thriving homes but also prove ourselves in the world. Stay-at-home moms struggle with this in their own ways, but for working moms, we, like Willy and most other male characters in American drama, may wonder if what we do for a living is impressive enough. After putting extensive time and effort into something, it's natural to view it as an extension of ourselves in some way. However, though Willy is not able to hack it at work, ultimately letting professional declined define him as a person, our challenge is not just doing the job well but being willing to set boundaries to keep our job from hurting our homelife. Apparently, such musings are not the stuff of great literature. The classic plays show men and women in stereotypical roles where the man is the breadwinner and the woman is the bread baker. But each time I teach *Death of a Salesman*, I'm reminded of how I'm a mixture of Linda and Willy, and probably many of the young women reading it for my class are as well. Perhaps if such a character had been written, the play wouldn't have been a tragedy.

 As we gain insights through experience and trial by fire, we as working moms can help encourage fellow women going through similar

---

19. Miller, *Death of a Salesman*, 262.

things. Collectively, the church can prioritize family flourishing by little and big actions individuals choose to do in the workplace to support working moms. I've gone on maternity leave twice. We timed it perfectly over summer break for two pregnancies and needed about a month of maternity leave before or after summer with two pregnancies. I experienced support from my department as men and women colleagues stepped up to cover my classes while I was away. People at work have thrown me baby showers, and I've hosted showers for them. I've babysat for a colleague who needed some quiet time to work on PhD coursework, and an office manager has helped watch my child on a day where her school was closed. I've had a student (who was also a young mom) struggle with childcare, and one of my sweet fellow instructors volunteered to babysit for her during class several times until she was able to secure a sitter. Normalizing the challenges of being a working mom, modeling for younger women, and supporting fellow moms are all ways we can function as the body of Christ, uplifting and encouraging one another. I've gone into a family-owned business and seen a child still on winter break spread out in the back room with toys while his mom worked the cash register. We need to validate parents who remind us of our responsibility to do right by our employers or businesses and our families. We need to acknowledge that children are part of our lives and that there are times their world coincides with the workplace. This is something we should do as women, but it is also something we should welcome men to participate in as well.

So, wherever you are, I urge you to consider whether you are at peace, and if you're not, what can change. If you're feeling less than, especially compared to colleagues who are achieving more professionally, remember that creating boundaries at work allows for you to have more time and energy to be a homemaker. Sometimes when I feel overwhelmed at the huge task that being a working homemaker is, I remind myself, "I'm running a household." This is a big deal. Synonyms for homemaker like *domestic engineer* or *family manager* highlight how much being a homemaker really does require. Engineering and managing the inner and outer workings of a family and a household is an entire job in and of itself, and because of this, we ought to be gracious with ourselves when we prioritize doing this well and also performing well at our place of employment. We don't have to achieve everything possible professionally to be a good worker and a good example to young women who are watching. If you're overwhelmed because you have a job that does not complement well with your family's needs, I'm going to go against society's mindset and Hollywood's movies, which say you can make it all work if you just think positively. Jobs with flexibility are out there. You're not expecting too much to pursue one. Flexibility will not be unlimited, and even if it is, that can become a limitation as well, but mothers are starting to change the culture regarding work expectations by voicing our needs. Though we are influenced by the world we live in, we can also influence the world to better adjust to the well-being of families. Pope Pius XII rightly said, "The family is not made for society; Rather it is society which is made for the family."[20] In the long run, what is good for families is good for everyone.

---

20. Pope Pius XII, "Allocution to the Fathers of Families."

3

Let Him Parent, Not Just Play and Provide

"A good father is one of the most unsung, unpraised, unnoticed and yet one of the most valuable assets in our society."[1]

—Billy Graham

VERY EARLY ON, CHILDREN learn about "mom jobs" and "dad jobs." Traditional roles such as mom as the meal maker and dad as the car fixer connect to many people's natural tendencies, such as men being more likely to be interested in mechanics and women being more likely to want influence over our children's nutritional intake. Yet, there are sometimes unique family dynamics based on individual interests and schedule needs. One of the benefits of a working dad and stay-at-home mom setup is that the responsibilities are usually somewhat clearly defined. Dad takes care of work-related things, and mom takes care of home-related things. Of course, the fact that mom doesn't clock out at the end of the day usually means that her tasks continue into the evenings, as well as weekends and holidays. What many working moms have discovered is that because we are not superwoman, we cannot do everything required at work and everything required at home and still

---

1. Billy Graham Evangelistic Association.

have energy to be healthy and happy. But many of us are still trying. Though most of this book is for working mamas of all sorts, this chapter specifically relates to working mothers in dual-income marriages. If you are divorced or your husband stays home, this chapter will not speak to your immediate situation, though it may in a different life season. The Pew Research Center conducted a study in 2023 and found what most of us probably already know: in marriages where the wife works, she still does the bulk of the housework. Husbands of working wives "spend about 3.5 hours more per week on leisure activities than wives do. Wives in these marriages spend roughly 2 hours more per week on caregiving than husbands do and about 2.5 hours more on housework."[2] The *second shift*[3] is the term for the unpaid labor that working women do at home after their workday is completed.

In her satirical essay "I Want a Wife," Judy (Syfers) Brady famously highlighted the unreasonable expectations that can be placed upon mothers who do everything.[4] Brady wrote the essay from a woman's perspective. She is not a lesbian, but she wrote about wanting a wife to make the point that she wanted someone to assist her with the myriad of tasks that wives are responsible for. Brady wrote the essay as an irritated feminist, pointing out patriarchy's shortcomings. This is not the approach I intend to take. There is value in being a homemaker. There is sanctification in serving our family. However, despite the love we have for our families and the dedication we have for our work, we can burn ourselves out by trying to do everything for everyone. Thinking it is possible to do it all can become a sort of pride in which we believe we are the only ones capable of taking care of needs at home.

Christians are somewhat divided regarding whether they believe in gender complementarianism or gender egalitarianism. The first means that men and women were created to hold different roles that complement one another and that there is a biblical hierarchy of male headship. The second means that men and women are intended to hold the same roles and there should be no hierarchy; examples of male headship in the Bible are viewed as specific to the culture of that time or

2. Fry et al., "In a Growing Share."
3. Hochschild and Machung, *The Second Shift*.
4. Brady (Syfers), "I Want a Wife."

LET HIM PARENT, NOT JUST PLAY AND PROVIDE

consequences of the fall. If you are a complementarian, please consider that asking your husband to help with your children and home does not overstep his leadership. In fact, verses in the Bible about the husband leading the home never specify who should do which household duties. I believe there is a biblical basis for men to be leaders and protectors, but husbands can enact that role in a variety of ways. Men are called to be leaders in their homes, but that leadership does not somehow remove them from serving their family in domestic ways. In fact, true leaders are servants who lead by example. Galatians 5:13 tells us to "serve one another humbly in love." This applies equally to men and women.

For those of us who value homemaking, we will likely take on the bulk of domestic duties naturally. Part of this is our desire to care for our family. Part of it may be the need we feel to prove (to others and maybe even ourselves) that we are being good wives and mothers. Yet there may be some cumbersome and unnecessary aspects of homemaking that I have only myself to blame for. If I insist on having ten throw pillows on the couches, but they end up on the floor 75 percent of the time, that's on me. I can be irritated with Ben for walking past them rather than fluffing and repositioning, but he would be happy to just get rid of the pillows. Sometimes we put expectations on ourselves about how our homes needs to look or function that are unnecessary and can even lead to strife. For example, in our home, I like to make our kids' birthdays as special as I can. I decorate the night before so that the kids will wake up surprised and happy on their big day. Ben usually helps me pretty willingly, but there are times he is less than enthused. What I've had to remind myself is that decorating according to a theme at 9 p.m. at night is by no means a criteria for being a good parent or a good homemaker. It's something I like to do, but if Ben does not, I should be grateful for his help rather than assuming that he owes it to me. In these sorts of situations where we take on unnecessary duties for the sake of being Pinterest worthy, we should not expect our husbands, or anyone else for that matter, to share in our vision. However, when we are drowning in chores and our husbands are home and available to help, it's okay to ask.

I know, I know; we don't want to have to ask. We want them to magically notice the stress we are feeling and offer to help. But men are not wired to pick up on cues as easily as women, so sometimes they won't without a little nudge. Research from a Harvard psychologist confirms that "women read people with greater accuracy" and that they are "more responsive to nonverbal cues than men."[5] Yet, the truth is good men want to be there for their wives and children. They may not notice our busyness or think of offering on their own, but they would rather have us ask for help when we need it than secretly resent them for not helping. A study conducted by Pew Research Center found that 77 percent of people believed that in homes where the mom and dad both work, they should focus equally on their jobs and the household.[6] This means that most people believe that women and men should both help with childcare and housework. But beliefs only change into actions when we are a part of the necessary forward motion. Asking for help can take humility. We want to be able to do it all, so asking for a hand is a recognition of our need. A quote that comes to mind is, "Just because someone carries it well doesn't mean it isn't heavy." The idea is that sometimes a need is hidden because the person copes so well. As working homemakers, we have learned how to balance a lot and often do it pretty well. Yet this may mask, even to our spouses and maybe ourselves, the needs we have. This quote is often specified to women, changing it to, "Just because *she* carries it well . . ." This is likely because it is indeed women who tend to silently carry our burdens. Letting our husbands know our load is heavy does not mean we are not capable, but it is a way to let our husbands love us. If we are trying to manage the laundry, dinner, baths, homework, and school lunches for the next day all at once, we aren't failing by asking for help. We are being human.

Eve, as we know, was created to be Adam's helpmate. They were equal in value, and neither were meant to bear a burden alone. Adam needed assistance and companionship, but Eve was not created to do it all for him. She is referenced as a helper through the Hebrew word *ezer*. This word is also used when the Scripture references God as our helper: "The LORD is on my side as my *ezer*" (Psalm 118:7).[7] God is not our servant, but through his help we can accomplish things we otherwise could not do. Similarly, in a healthy marriage, each spouse should assist

---

5. Nelson, "Differences in Nonverbal Cues."
6. Fry et al., "In a Growing Share."
7. Stackhouse, *Partners in Christ*, 82.

LET HIM PARENT, NOT JUST PLAY AND PROVIDE

the other in accomplishing what he or she could not do alone. Women were created to serve alongside men, but some women have gotten the message that we are to subjugate ourselves at the expense of our own well-being. This is not only unbiblical, but it also hurts the entire family, for if the mama is not functioning healthily, it will not be long before the rest of the family follows suit.

We likely handle our work responsibilities without assistance from our husbands. However, the home is a shared space that both a husband and wife need to be invested in. Although men may not typically value nurturing in the same way women do, husbands are instructed to love their wives and to interact with us in ways that lead to our flourishing. First Peter 3:7 says, "Husbands, in the same way be considerate as you live with your wives, and treat them with respect as the weaker partner and as heirs with you of the gracious gift of life, so that nothing will hinder your prayers." I'll be honest: I hate the thought of being weak. In many ways, we as women are so strong. We've given birth; we're keeping tiny (or not so tiny anymore) humans alive; we're navigating working and homemaking, and the list goes on. But acknowledging my own limitations reminds me of my need for God and my need for my husband. It's okay to say we need our husbands; they need us too, otherwise Eve would not have been created for Adam. Women have been weaker in social status historically, and in some ways and places around the world, still are today. Usually, we are weaker physically in the sense that we have less body mass and muscle. This does not make us lesser, but it goes without saying that fine china requires different treatment than Fiestaware. However, women are also precious because of our internal state. We are complicated beings with so much happening internally. Women are three times more likely to suffer from mental health problems than men.[8] Physiological complications due to hormones can sometimes impact things. The author of *The Female Brain* reports, "[M]ore and more neuroscientists are finding that sensitivity to fear, stress, genes, estrogen, progesterone, and innate brain biology play important roles."[9] However, circumstances also impact our internal state and "psychologists have emphasized cultural and social explanations

---

8. Mental Health Foundation, "Men and Women: Statistics."
9. Brizendine. *Female Brain*, 132.

for this 'depression gender gap.'"[10] We may be carrying too much. We may be shouldering responsibilities we were never meant to bear alone.

There is a persistent myth that women multitask better than men. Study after study has disproven this,[11] but the myth continues. Why? Because women continue to believe that we can or should juggle everything. We may not even let our husbands try to help. Many husbands really think their wives do multitask well, despite the fact no one is good at it, and grow accustomed to an ingrained pattern. This has a consequence, though. Working mothers specifically struggle with mental health. A recent study confirms that "more working mothers have been diagnosed with anxiety and/or depression (42%) than the general population (28%), their coworkers without kids (25%) and even working fathers (35%). Working mothers were also more likely to report that their mental health had worsened in the last year (33%)."[12] These numbers are alarming. They suggest that not only do we need to make hard decisions about the work environment we engage with, but we also need to make thoughtful decisions about our family dynamics and whether our homemaking is allowing everyone, ourselves included, to thrive.

This idea that to be a mother is to lose yourself to self-sacrifice has been acknowledged (and criticized) for some time, though it does not make the issue any less relevant. Every couple years, I teach the late-nineteenth-century American novel *The Awakening*, by Kate Chopin. It is the story of Edna Pontellier and her quest to find purpose and identity outside of the roles of being a wife and a mother. In the end, she does not believe there is any answer to her questions of how to mother well without being subsumed by the role, so she commits suicide, walking into the ocean, from which she will never return. Here is a poignant line from Edna that is as haunting as it is beautiful: "I would give up the unessential; I would give up my money, I would give my life for my children; but I wouldn't give myself."[13] What she means is she would make any sacrifice for her children that would allow her to maintain

---

10. Brizendine. *Female Brain*, 132.

11. "Why Multitasking Doesn't Work" and Liu et al., "Effects of Working Memory Capacity, Task Switching, and Task Difficulty on Multitasking Performance."

12. CVS Health, "Mental Health Crisis of Working Moms."

13. Chopin, *Awakening*, 53.

some autonomy apart from being a caregiver. What Edna finds is that others only see her through her connections to her family, which she resents. While Edna loves her children, she is overwhelmed with her life. I would diagnose Edna as suffering from anxiety and depression but also unrealistic expectations. Before her decision to take her own life, Edna is undoubtedly selfish; she lives lavishly and thinks about her own happiness far above that of others, her family included. However, she is also an example of a woman who is unable to resist ideas about what a good wife and mother should look like according to the standard of other people rather than trying to create a homelife that makes sense for the needs of her family and the life she wants to lead. Kate Chopin did not criticize mothers for facing challenges in motherhood, but she criticized the idea that mothers must be ever-sacrificing, never-tiring people. Edna is far from a good mother. Yet, this fictional character is a good reminder of our need to live as mothers in ways that allow flourishing rather than thinking that our roles as a wife and mother will always be at odds with our own well-being. Edna felt stifled by her home, but this should have been her safe place.

Homes should be a refuge from the outside world. I remember being a busy teenager in high school. I often had activities that kept me occupied during the week and even some weekends. But once in a while, there was nothing planned on a Friday night, and my mom would order a Casey's pizza (which was a treat; we rarely ate out or got takeout) and let us watch some sitcoms together as a family. I looked forward to that night all week and still remember the feeling of comfort from enjoying being together that those moments evoked. Friday is still my favorite day of the week because of the way we prioritize being together at home, which started when I was young. But when I think back on it, what also made those Friday nights so special was that my mom would sit down and just be with us. She was often cleaning, meal prepping, or completing some other chore. On these Friday nights, though, she would let herself stop and spend some quality time with us, and that is really what helped make the nights so special.

We can create the most inviting atmosphere for our children and husbands regarding activities, food, and ambiance, but if we are frazzled and not able to just be with our family, it will not have the same impact.

My personal go-to when I'm upset that Ben is not helping me enough is to give him the silent treatment (mature, I know). I won't yell or pick a fight, but I will ignore him. Inevitably, though, I end up punishing myself as well as him when it would have been much easier and effective to just ask him to vacuum. Overall, I have gotten better at asking and, because of this, he has also gotten better at offering. Though I like to be the one to oversee our schedule and do most of the household chores, the freedom in asking Ben to pick up kids when I have a meeting or study with our daughter while I pack lunches not only reduces my stress, but it also releases me from feeling resentment. This need to share each other's burdens is relevant for all families, not just dual-income families.

Too often our society interprets *mothering* as micromanaging and *fathering* as siring. Both are incorrect. Mothering and fathering should include caring, teaching, and equipping. The biblical model of husbands loving their wives and wives respecting their husbands (Ephesians 5:33) is so relevant to the way we manage household duties. It is not very loving for a husband to be on his phone most of the night while his wife never gets a chance to rest until bedtime. Neither is it very respectful for a wife to view her husband as her personal assistant and to expect her every whim on a "honey do" list to be addressed immediately. This beautiful and complicated and messy thing of being in a sacred union like marriage requires us to constantly grow and be curious about one another's needs. What works for a couple when they get married will likely need to be tweaked (or completely revamped) as they welcome children. In our earlier years, when I had a modified schedule at work, I went to work later and stayed later on certain days, which meant Ben picked up the kids and made dinner at least two nights a week. Now I work typical hours, and I cook most of the time because I'm home first. I have found that it's important to be flexible in what works and be willing to change it as things develop into a new season. Your marriage doesn't have to look like everyone else's. If you prefer to mow the grass and he prefers to do the laundry, that's great. As one wise theologian puts it, "The liberty here is to do whatever makes the most of the particular gifts, desires, opportunities, and needs of the individuals that make up that family, without simplistically sorting things according to sex."[14] What is

---

14. Stackhouse, *Partners in Christ*, 119.

important is that neither feels resentment for carrying too much of the load or being unappreciated for their contribution.

The default mode of moms doing the bulk of the work at home has been promoted by media portraying fathers as incompetent. Although men are often shown as savvy businessmen or workers on screen, when it comes to their role at home, they are shown to be incapable, unwise, and basically there for comic relief. As one article puts it, "Buffoonish, ignorant, self-centered, and inept television dads must be shown their proper places in the home . . . at worst, they are relegated to the intellectual level of the family pet."[15] Earlier cartoons like *The Flinstones* and *The Simpsons* do this, as do sitcoms ranging from *Family Matters* and *Everybody Loves Raymond* to *According to Jim*. However, more recent shows are often no better (*Good Luck Charlie* and *Modern Family*). These negative portrayals very likely influence cultural beliefs about masculinity and fatherhood.[16]

Ideas such as dads babysitting their own children suggest that dads are only a fill-in for mom and they do not (and should not) have any real responsibility for their children and the household. These ideas are poisoning homes by leading to overworked moms and disrespected dads. Despite a father's love for the Lord, he will not be seen as wise in spiritual ways if he is not already seen as competent in practical ways. Ephesians 6:4 says, "Fathers, do not exasperate your children; instead, bring them up in the training and instruction of the Lord." Fathers can only successfully bring their children up if they are present and respected. The way we treat our husbands and the way we ask for help from them have an impact on the way our children perceive their dads. If we accuse them of being lazy and fight with them about their lack of involvement in front of our children, we diminish our husbands' desire to interact and invalidate their importance. It is necessary for us to communicate our need for their help, but we should do so lovingly and, at times, privately. Purposing not to criticize each other in front of the kids helps set an example for the way our children should treat us and each other and it also holds us accountable for not disrespecting our spouses. If we wait

---

15. McGee, "Portrayal of Fathers," 36.
16. McGee, "Portrayal of Fathers," 39.

until the kids are asleep to address it, very likely emotions have settled, and we will be able to discuss more courteously.

The common jab that when mom is gone, the kids and house fall apart under dad's watch may seem to be all in good fun, but it can cause resentment in wives and apathy in husbands, which impacts the quality of our marriages. A recent study shows that women initiate almost 70 percent of divorces.[17] One law firm speculates why: "When women excel at their careers, are expected to perform more of the domestic duties, and don't get support from their husbands, well, it's no wonder women initiate divorce more often. They may, quite simply, determine that being married is no longer in their best interest."[18] While I understand that some divorces are unavoidable due to toxic situations, it is heartbreaking that the most sacred relationship God has blessed us with is being called something that is not in women's best interest. Marriage is not only a gift for couples, but research proves it is an influential factor in children's well-being.[19] Our homes, our children, and our marriages are worth fighting for. When we feel overworked and unsupported by our husbands, we need to let them know. They are not mind readers. Things might need to change at home and these changes may be hard work, but recognizing the need for change is a good thing because it can lead to hope and progress. The number one indicator for overall life satisfaction is not career related; it is the quality of one's marriage.[20] We must prioritize our marriages if we want to have fulfilled lives and be the best version of ourselves for our children. Letting our husbands know what we need for our marriages to be healthy is wise, not selfish.

The irony is that although children are a result of our relationships with our husbands, they are also often what strain our marriages. Surveys have found that satisfaction in marriage goes down after kids come along, despite the love parents have for their children.[21] This marriage dissatisfaction undoubtedly relates to the heavy workload moms face

---

17. American Sociological Association, quoted in Jimenez Law Firm, "Why Women Initiate Divorce."

18. Jimenez Law Firm, "Why Women Initiate Divorce."

19. Ribar, "Why Marriage Matters."

20. Diener et al., "Subjective Well-Being"; Norval and Weaver, "Contribution of Marital Happiness."

21. Doss, "Effect of the Transition to Parenthood."

running the household, along with the way the practicalities of parenting can zap the romance. So, the way we manage our families must support our marriages rather than detract from them. Life will always be somewhat hectic; there will always be a degree of stress. But we can have fulfilling marriages in which we feel supported by our husbands and like-minded in our understanding of the need to share household responsibilities. It not only lightens our load, but it also allows our husbands to lead in our homes, and it allows our children to see their fathers as capable not just at work but in the very space they occupy with them.

A mother's sacrifice is a pretty well known (though maybe less well appreciated.) However, in marriages where husbands share in home responsibilities, we should also recognize their sacrifices. Especially for couples where the husband and wife both work, there may be a sacrifice regarding a man's worldly success. I've already talked about the sacrifices that being a working homemaker may require. However, husbands who support their working wives may also have to accept career limitations. High-achieving men in the workforce typically have stay-at-home wives or wives who do not work full-time, which allows them to focus more on work while their wives handle things at home. Research confirms this in executive roles, college president roles, and the highest-earning roles (also known as the 1 percent).[22] Though many husbands (mine included) may not necessarily desire optimal career achievement, I find it helpful to remind myself that my husband's support of our family and my career may place limitations on his. He shares taking off sick days with me to watch an unwell child and handles homework and bedtime on the occasional nights I need to be at a school event. And this embracement of his role at home, this rejection of how the world views successful masculinity, is an act of love from him that adds to the well-being of our family and better enables me to contribute to the common good.

Initiating healthy shared levels of responsibility not only refines both husbands and wives but it helps our marriages and can positively impact our children's future marriages. Girls raised by dual working parents are more likely to work themselves and have less ambivalence about

---

22. Seltzer, "Gender Roles and Presidential Spouses"; Groysberg and Abrahams, "Manage Your Work"; Yavorsky, "Separate Spheres."

how to make such an arrangement work. Boys raised by dual working parents grow up to be fathers who help more with household chores and child-rearing.[23] It may feel like the kindest thing to do is to bear the weight of running the household alone, but we are only human. Our best intentions to be self-sacrificing can lead to burnout if we do not recognize our limits, work with our husbands to create shared responsibilities, and model self-care for our benefit and the rest of our family's benefit. *Self-care* can mean a lot of different things today. It can be an excuse for a bubble bath, sweet treat, or shopping spree. However, true self-care is not temporarily finding an escape but finding a way to manage and find satisfaction in long-term situations. For example, many of us may prefer taking turns sleeping in on Saturday morning to receiving a diamond bracelet. Sometimes the ways our husbands think we want to be honored is different than the restorative self-care that helps us be at our best as wives and mothers. Working moms often have a limited social life. Because we're away from our children when we work, we may want to be with our children the rest of the time (and even if we'd like some socialization, we often feel guilty about it.) Yet, we need to create relationships with other women. Letting yourself attend a Bible study or go out for coffee with a girlfriend can be a form of self-care. It's our responsibility to convey what we need. If you're feeling overwhelmed and don't know what you need, it's worth figuring that out.

    Our husbands would likely rather help and have a healthy wife (physically, mentally, and emotionally) than be uninvolved at home and have a wife who is unhappy and perhaps even unwell. We often determine certain tasks that are gender neutral as being feminine, but King David (from the Old Testament) is an excellent example of ways that a man can have a variety of interests and be involved in a variety of tasks without handing in his man card. David was a harpist, a poet, and a dancer as well as a mighty warrior. My husband has changed his share of diapers and played Polly Pocket with the girls, but he also gets his hands dirty under the hood of our minivan. He bathes our children, and he shovels the driveway. And I find that sexy. (In fact, I'm not the only one. Research from Cornell University says that men who help

---

23. Nobel, "Kids Benefit."

LET HIM PARENT, NOT JUST PLAY AND PROVIDE

with household chores have sex with their wives more often.[24]) The idea of a man being "whipped" if he helps at home could not be more incorrect about what makes a real man. If we believe that women can do well in the workplace, the natural conclusion is that men are also capable of doing domestic things well.

Although I am encouraging shared responsibility in the home, this does not mean we should expect our husbands to be our minions and do our bidding just as we would do it. We need to give them our trust and get rid of perfectionist beliefs that things can only be done one way. When I needed to attend a late-night work event recently, I asked Ben if he could pack the kids' lunches for school the next day. I admit that when I came home, I was tempted to criticize his decision to put everything in baggies rather than use the lunchbox Tupperware. I was also tempted to criticize his decision to make PB&J sandwiches *and* pack trail mix, which also includes peanuts. But the truth is, the lunches were made; they contained vegetables and nutritional value, and my load was lessoned by not having to pack lunches after a busy day. Our methods of managing the kids may look different from the way our husbands do it, but there is a vast difference between co-parenting and commandeering how we want our husbands to parent. (I'm only recommending the former.) Just as women bring specific strengths to the workplace that are lacking if we are not there, men bring specific strengths to our homes. They bring fun and creativity. Our way of loading the dishwasher is not the only way to do it. There are some important big-picture structures that couples should be on the same page about: screen time, appropriate friends, bedtime, homework requirements, and the like. But all the details of how such things can happen will look different from family to family and from mom to dad. I have learned to accept the fact that when I am out of town, Ben and the kids will go out to eat at least once. Bedtime will be a little later, and the house may not be as clean. But my rigidness in getting the kids ready for bed at 7:40 p.m. on the dot doesn't make me a better parent—it just shows my high need for a structured schedule. On the other hand, when I take the kids for a walk, I'm usually okay with them running (or rolling) ahead as long as I can still see them. Ben is not; this shows his need to ensure the kids' safety. Men who value

---

24. Kelley, "Want More Sex?"

their involvement in their homes have agency in their role. We can't say we want our husbands to be leaders in our homes and then criticize them for everything they do. The idea of a "henpecked" husband is not what any of us desire, but that means we need to let go of impulses to micromanage. If our husbands grocery shop, we need to be okay with them possibly buying a different brand or veering from the list. Our way is not the only way.

So, practically speaking, what does sharing the household load mean? It might not mean fifty-fifty for everyone, especially if your husband works more hours, but it should mean something that is manageable for both of you as a couple. Also, there are plenty of home chores that extend beyond the house. In our marriage, Ben handles all the outdoor maintenance. He mows, landscapes, and cares for the vehicles. Part of this is due to our preferences. He loves being outside, and I like the outdoors . . . in moderation, but would prefer to do chores in air conditioning or heat, depending on the season. Because we own over an acre, he is very busy with lawn maintenance from the spring until the fall, so I do most of the house cleaning and meal prep then, and he steps in as I need him to. For example, he always pitches in when we have company coming and need to make the house extra tidy, and he prepares meals on nights I take the kids to activities. Yet, I often find myself growing a little resentful in the cold winter months when he has almost no outdoor responsibilities and my house chores are the same. So, I usually ask for more help when he is not busy doing other things, which works well because this is often when there are holiday-related tasks or events filling up the schedule. Our system is not perfect, and we still have to work on communicating so neither of us feels overworked or taken for granted, but finding what works for your marriage and your family will help you feel united in your parenting.

I'd like to share a little scenario from years ago that shows a practical, and humbling, example of how trying to single-handedly navigate everything can go south. I like to have my kids take yearly photos, documenting an official picture of each age. Often, we'll have the photographer snap some family photos too. Ben hates this ritual with a passion. I can't blame him. Preparing for pictures is a whole thing, and he doesn't like being in front of or behind cameras. So, I essentially asked him

LET HIM PARENT, NOT JUST PLAY AND PROVIDE

to just show up, in an effort to minimize his loathing of said pictures. For one of these milestone family photo sessions, I made sure everyone had clean, cute, coordinating clothes. I got everyone fed and napped in time to make it to the studio and back before anyone had a meltdown. We only had the two girls at that point, but life could still get hectic. I made an effort getting myself ready but gave most of my attention, as usual, to the girls. After we took the photos, the photographer told me our package came with a free 8x10 photo, so I chose a family picture. It wasn't until I got the pictures back that, after oohing and aahing at the girls' cuteness, I noticed a black speck on one of my teeth. I figured it was a flaw on the picture paper, but when I tried to wipe it off, it wouldn't budge. After looking through all the photos, I realized that I had been so focused on making sure the girls were happy and presentable that I hadn't had time to brush my teeth after quickly eating something, much less take a careful look in the mirror. Needless to say, that 8x10 has never seen the light of day, let alone a frame. Why neither Ben nor the photographer saw the problem and gave me a heads-up is still a mystery, but I've come to see this little family photo faux pas as a lighthearted example of a serious truth. We can't do it all well, and when we try, even if all the plates keep spinning, there is a cost. It would be nice if someone else were able to accurately assess the situation and give us a big, "Hey, you've got some broccoli in your teeth." But even those who walk through life with us do not always catch the signs that our attempt to be servant-hearted and sacrificial can backfire.

Society has come a long way from the 1950s model of a mom holding down the fort at home and dad arriving for dinner and TV time. Dads today are spending more time with their children than fathers of previous generations.[25] It's common to see dads wearing babies and pushing strollers, something that our grandmothers and even mothers didn't experience as young wives. We should celebrate these strides, but the next step is what happens in homes behind closed doors. Things have gotten better—today's dads do "twice the housework, compared to fathers a generation ago."[26] But studies still show that although fathers are present more than they used to be, in most homes, mamas are still

---

25. Renner, "Fathers Today More Engaged."
26. Behson, *Working Dad's Survival Guide*, foreword.

doing the bulk of the work. I don't say this because we should demand equality and respect. As Christians, we should be willing to humble ourselves and to serve our families and others. Yet, divorce rates and spikes in mental illness in working mothers suggest that it is not healthy to try to do it all. Homemaking is not just about hot meals, folded laundry, and an organized calendar. It's about an atmosphere of love and respect. It's about a place where all members of the family can enjoy themselves and their time together. Loving marriages are not about guilting or punishing the other person to do what we want, but they are about voicing our needs to our spouses. We don't want to be married to Mr. Mom, and it's good to remember how our husbands' masculinity adds to our homes. But it is also worth recognizing that we are not failing in being homemakers if we ask for help. Our husbands can only help us remove the metaphorical food from our teeth if we have let them know we want their input and value their involvement. Self-care is family care.

4

Less Is More

> "Busyness is not godliness. God is not impressed with your production capacity as much as He is concerned that the product of your home—your own children—be chiseled and molded and perfected to the best of your ability."
>
> —Dorothy Patterson[1]

"Let's go—we're late" is an almost daily rallying crying for me during the school year as I direct my four children from their various play or primping places in the house to the minivan. We're not usually late—just close, as the typical morning business of snuggles and toothbrushes, buttoned shirts and missing shoes unfolds. If I could change one thing about our school-year schedule, I think it would be the morning. No matter how much earlier I get up than them, even though the backpacks and lunch boxes are already loaded before they wake, the natural slow morning pace of my kids makes the mornings a little rushed. But it is also because of this unavoidable need for timeliness that I am reminded to work against a rushed schedule. I cannot change the time that school begins, but I can decide how many activities we fill our schedule with, how many demands we allow upon our free hours.

---

1. Patterson, *Handbook for Ministers' Wives*, 104.

The Working Homemaker

Time is truly a precious and scarce resource. It's a sobering fact that during the school week, my children spend more of their awake time away from me than with me. This is why it is so important for me to guard the time that I have with my family. The term *hygge* has become popular lately. It is often used to describe cozy decorating styles, but it can be much more. According to Jamie Erickson in her book *Holy Hygge*, although hygge as an ambiance mantra or self-help doctrine will fall short, hygge as a philosophy can help believers engage in purposeful commitments. Though she is not specifically talking about motherhood, her definition of hygge describes the mindset I desire to create for my family: "Hygge is the opposite of hustle. It eschews overabundance. It savors. It takes things slow and envelops in sanctuary."[2] This hygge mentality is countercultural. In a world that validates busyness, it suggests that we slow down. This makes perfect sense as a child-rearing practice. Time moves quickly even if our days do not. People say things like "Don't blink or you'll miss it" for a reason. I don't find it helpful to use the passage of time as way to guilt ourselves. But recognizing its unavoidable impact should cause us to choose our activities wisely. The psalmist reminds us, "Be still, and know that I am God" (Psalm 46:10) because it is so easy to forget the importance of stillness and non-busyness, though this is exactly what we need to orient ourselves and our families heavenward.

Twenty-first-century America is an advanced society, so you won't see people going around worshipping pagan golden images; nevertheless, we have our idols. In this chapter, I'm going to talk about two: the idol of busyness and the idol of talents. I'm sure we've all noticed that in catching up with someone and learning what she has been up to, acknowledging busyness is one of the first things covered. It's almost a bragging right. If we are not busy, it is easy to think (or worry that other people will think) that we are boring, unpopular, or lazy. The only thing worse than people thinking this about us is people thinking this about our children. To avoid this, kids today are involved in a large variety of activities. Ranging from karate to musical theater or from debate club to kids' ministry, there are any number of options for a family to choose from.

---

2. Erickson, *Holy Hygge*, 15.

Just to be clear, I am not against enrichment; I'm actually all for it. But as is true for most things in life, even things that are good in moderation can become a problem in excess. (Did you know you can become overhydrated, despite all the benefits of drinking water?)[3] So, let's start with the reasons to get our kids involved in extracurriculars. Good grades—they often lead to future academic goals.[4] Socialization—it gives them the chance to meet kids and interact with mentors. Confidence—it gives them the ability to learn something new and likely demonstrate it in front of others. Skill—they can gain aptitude at something. Commitment—it teaches them to stick with something. Time management—it teaches them how to balance school along with other activities. Future opportunities—acceptance and scholarships at desirable colleges can be influenced by extracurricular involvement. Clearly, there are many reasons to be encouraged, or feel obligated, to get our kids involved in a variety of activities. Besides all that, there is simply peer pressure. Everybody else's kids are doing things, so shouldn't ours be too? And that pressure starts early. Mommy-and-me classes are offered for toddlers, and the pattern of scheduling our children continues from there.

However, the downside is that many of the positive reasons parents involve their kids in activities in the first place often backfire. Trying every sport will not ensure that a child will find one he likes or become good at it. Starting an activity does not ensure buy-in. Although commitment is often a desired outcome, according to Dr. Rosenfeld, by thirteen years of age, three out of four kids who started organized activities young drop out after a few years.[5] Also, many of the character qualities or life skills we want our children to learn are not exclusive to specific activities. Kids can learn confidence, commitment, and time management in a variety of ways, not just through extracurriculars. Though this does not make the activities inherently bad, if this is the only reason we are doing them, it's not very strong logic. I've heard parents say they involve their children in a time (and money) intensive activity because it will teach them how to deal with failure. This is a commendable goal.

3. Semeco, "What Happens if You Drink Too Much Water?"
4. Mayol-García, "Children Continue."
5. Kirchheimer, "Overscheduled Child."

I certainly want my children to know how to respond to failure and not to give up. However, life itself will afford ample opportunity for failure; I'm not sure I have to orchestrate and pay for opportunities for my kids to experience it.

We need to be honest with ourselves regarding why we are encouraging our kids to do all these things. Wanting to give our children experiences we didn't have but wish we did can be commendable but also gets tricky. Expecting our children to excel at something because we did is even trickier. It is normal for kids to gravitate toward things their parents enjoy. Our interests can be contagious, and shared interests allow for a family to have common ground and things they enjoy doing together. However, if we are more invested in the activity than our children are, that can become a problem. It can lead to resentment from them, which then becomes resentment from us when we are spending time and money on something they don't appreciate. So, is it ever okay to push our children to do something they don't want to do? I would say we need to examine our hearts and be honest with ourselves about why we want them to do it. If we are trying to live vicariously through our children, this is a red flag. If we expect them to be a carbon copy of us, this is another red flag.

There are times when we can see a greater good that our kids might not value at the time. We as parents need to be able to articulate why something is important to experience and then identify the level of competency we would like our child to achieve and consider why. For example, my girls are learning piano. They are going at a rather slow pace because lessons are only once a week, and they only practice a few times a week beyond that. (The pace picks up a bit in the summer, when we have more free time.) The slowness of their piano learning sometimes bothers me because I started playing young and was a music minor in college, achieving a high level of proficiency. But none of my girls have wanted to go at a faster pace. In fact, I often prod them. There are many activities about which I would never prod, but I value their learning how to read music and want them to be able to sit down at a piano and play a basic hymn or Christmas carol. However, my valuing it really is not enough to justify it. There are other important factors though.

Playing classical music helps brain functioning[6] and being able to sight read and play music from hymnals and common sheet music will come in handy throughout their lives. Playing the piano offers practical ways to honor the Lord through music and serve the community. But this does not mean my girls need to play Rachmaninoff or attend Juilliard. Though their progress is slow, if we are consistent over the years, I hope they will achieve competency without becoming burned out. Once they've achieved this level, I'll let them decide if they want to continue. However, not all valuable skills are achievable and practical for all kids. We as parents must often weigh our desires for our children with their own desires as well as their aptitude. If we find our kids are apt in many areas, we may have to guide them in the art of choosing.

Returning to my original idea about homemaking with hygge in mind, my main concern regarding extracurricular activities is the way it separates families and hurries schedules. This becomes even more important for families with working moms because we are with our children less. It's relevant for any family where the kids spend the day at school but especially for dual-working families because all the errands and chores must also fit into after-work/school hours, which is also potential family time. If you work a traditional schedule, late afternoon and evening hours are a sacred time when families that have been apart all day reconvene to share about their day and spend time together. Yet, most extracurricular activities happen during this same time frame. Even if you have a flexible schedule, if their father does not, activities cut into time with him. The average American family eats dinner together only three nights a week.[7] Typically, dinner is the only meal working parents can eat with their children, and this is becoming a rare occurrence. Put another way, according to a recent survey, typical American families spend thirty-seven minutes of quality time together a day.[8] Not only do many kids spend evenings, as well as the day, away from their parents, but they spend it away from their siblings too, for most activities are divided by age and grade. Siblings have different activities on various nights at various times, and dinner becomes something eaten

---

6. "The Role of Music in Brain Development."
7. Hartman Group, "Desires, Barriers and Directions."
8. Thompson, "Families Only Spend 37 Minutes Together."

on the run as each person has time. Even spiritually enriching activities can take away from family time. Wednesday is the typical night for children and youth programing at most churches, but there may be additional nights for worship practice or other ministries.

It can be so easy to feel like we are being pulled in two different directions: one in which we want our children to have experiences and learn new things, and the other in which we know deep down that they need time just to be at home to bond with family and unwind. I have decided that if I am going to err, I am going to err on the side of under-scheduling. I have arrived at this conclusion due to a few considerations. One is my own disposition. I get overwhelmed when I have been at work all day and then must rush through dinner (even if it's a packed sandwich) to chauffeur my children somewhere. So, we do minimal activities for set periods of time (more on this later) because I don't function well when I'm overbooked, and "when mama ain't happy, ain't nobody happy."

Another factor is my top values. I value creativity and contentment, and overscheduled kids usually struggle to entertain themselves because they are so used to being told what to do. Our kids need to find ways to entertain themselves and to undertake projects and activities they don't have time to do if their schedules are too full. Because my children are in a traditional school setting where they sit at desks for a good portion of the day and are asked to be quiet, I value giving them opportunities to be unstructured and even noisy. To maintain order, many extracurricular activities are rigid. While there is a reason for this, it prolongs the time in which kids must be largely silent, wait in line, and follow directions. The importance of play is relevant for all children, not just the very young. Dr. Battles says it well: "Many adults are continually overscheduling children and keeping the lives of these kids so structured that free play is an afterthought. But the need for play to ignite creativity is real. Children need time to play freely and this allows their creativity to flourish."[9]

More than being involved in every club and having exposure playing every sport or instrument, our children need to learn life skills like carrying on conversations and interacting with those both older and

9. Battles, *Let Them Play*, 4.

younger than themselves. When kids are separated into their own age group at school all day and then are again separated by age group for many extracurricular activities in the evenings, they don't practice interacting with those outside of their immediate peers. They are expected to act as others their age, regardless of ways they may be developing faster or slower in certain areas. We know our children and can help them in what is appropriate due to their personality and cognitive development, not just their age. Frederick Burk criticized grouping children solely according to age way back in 1921, saying it "is constructed upon the assumption that a group of minds can be marshalled and controlled in growth in exactly the same manner that a military officer marshalls and directs the bodily movements of a company of soldiers."[10] Creating margin in our life to be home with no agenda allows for our children to develop friendships with elderly neighbors, to engage with us, and to develop strong relationships with their siblings.

When I think about my own life, I've always loved to write. I've started doing more writing projects, such as this one, and, of course, I ended up being an English professor. But my parents never put me in creative writing classes or workshops. As a girl, I would write silly stories about animals. As a young teen, I remember lying face down in a rectangle of sunshine under the skylight in our living room and writing. I wrote plays that we performed at our church. I did this because I had free time to do something creative. It is easy to believe that we must see our children's talent and capitalize on it by directing them to activities that will help them flourish. But one of the best things we can do for our children's natural talents is give them margin in their day to discover their interests by expressing themselves in organic ways. Since my oldest daughter was young, we have had an activity table in the dining room supplied with paper and art supplies. It is amazing to see what all four of my children had concocted, of their own accord, at that table simply because it was there, and they were looking for something to do.

Of course, a child cannot teach himself how to play football or create pottery. There are specific skills that require a coach or teacher, but we don't have to "discover" our child. If someone has the talent to become the next star quarterback, he will naturally pick up a football;

---

10. Quoted in Silberman, *Crisis in the Classroom*, 166.

we shouldn't have to prod him to play. In scheduling our children's activities, in addition to natural aptitude, we should consider our end goal. Do we want them to learn to make pottery just to be creative, and if so, are there other ways to do this that better fit with our schedule than a weekly pottery class at dinnertime? Or is our child's goal to play sports in college, and for that to happen, does it require dedication and sacrifice during junior high and high school? Part of our job as parents is to allow our children to have experiences but not to give them unrealistic expectations. Few people grow up to be famous singers, actors, or athletes. Out of those who do, even fewer successfully lead happy lives with the burdens of fame and fortune. The tabloids remind us of this on a regular basis. Allowing our children to gain competency at something while acknowledging it is unlikely to directly affect their future career can help us maintain balance. It's okay to experience something for the sake of a hobby.

It is tempting to want our children to be good, even great, at things. This brings me to the idol of talents. We have probably all experienced that moment when we saw someone else's child doing something excellently and then looked over at our kid humming to herself and daydreaming. In a world that values productivity and output, we are constantly tempted to prove ourselves through our accomplishments. Social media encourages this. With the creation of LinkedIn, people now have a bona fide outlet for bragging about their educational and career success. But places like Facebook and Instagram are the stomping grounds for our kids' accomplishments. We are bombarded with notifications from parents about kids who are participating in recitals, winning sports championships, and the list goes on. The Lord recognizes our tendency to connect the big and impressive with the meaningful and worthwhile. Yet, he shows us time and again in his Word that part of his upside-down kingdom is doing things small and authentically. In assuring the prophet Elijah of his presence, during the time when Elijah was on the run for his life, trying to escape from wicked King Ahab, God did not appear in the powerful whirlwind, earthquake, or fire but instead appeared in a still small voice (1 Kings 19:11-12.) When Jesus began his ministry, he recruited a ragtag, motley crew of disciples rather than Sadducees or educated men well connected to the temple. The human heart will always be wowed by spectacle, but we serve a God who has modeled humbleness and called us to the same. This doesn't mean we cannot expose our children to experiences and help them cultivate skills. I have found it largely means searching my heart for my motivation in why our family does the things we do and being willing to say no to things that are normal or impressive in the world's eyes but do not enrich us as a family unit.

Wanting our children to be exceptional at something is understandable but can be harmful. Dr. Rosenfeld cautions, "The purpose of our children, simply stated, has become to make us proud and happy . . . we also look to our children to make us feel significant and fulfilled as human beings."[11] Our success as parents is not connected to what our kids can do but who they have been cultivated to be. Rather than teaching them that success comes through their accomplishments, I want to teach my children that fulfillment comes through confidence in who God has created us to be, embracing everyday moments and being available for spontaneous experiences that aren't possible when every moment is scheduled. G. K. Chesterton said, "The most extraordinary thing in the world is an ordinary man and an ordinary woman and their ordinary children."[12] A desire to create exceptionalism can cause us to miss what already has the potential of being extraordinary: a family who has time for each other and lives simply and faithfully. The apostle Paul encouraged believers to "make it your ambition to lead a quiet life" (1 Thessalonians 4:11). Such a life may not be impressive by the world's standards, but when we resist the noise and the chaos, we prioritize homemaking values for our family.

When our children moderately participate in an extracurricular activity, there will always be families who treat the activity as a priority, and this makes it tempting to increase our involvement. We find ourselves saying things like, "He can't enjoy it unless he's good at it. It's not fun to lose or be last." It can be easy to end up pursuing additional classes or private lessons/coaching for something that began just for fun. I try to remind myself that the purpose of childhood is not to master specific techniques; it is to be nourished and create bonds. They need

---

11. Rosenfeld and Wise, *Hyper-Parenting*, 143.
12. Chesterton, *Orthodoxy*.

time to play, sleep, and eat healthy food. They need time to be bored and practice creativity. Culture tells us to strive to be exceptional in quantifiable ways, but teaching our children contentment and curiosity in the natural world rather than relying too much on structed activities will serve them well. When I came across William Martin's poem "Do Not Ask Your Children to Strive," I felt like my desires for my family (which I sometimes second-guess in comparison to the accomplishments of others) were reaffirmed.

> Do not ask your children/to strive for extraordinary lives./Such striving may seem admirable,/but it is the way of foolishness./Help them instead to find the wonder/and the marvel of an ordinary life./Show them the joy of tasting/tomatoes, apples and pears./Show them how to cry/when pets and people die./Show them the infinite pleasure/in the touch of a hand./And make the ordinary come alive for them./The extraordinary will take care of itself.[13]

I love this poem because it affirms our role as parents in our children's lives. We are the ones who can teach them how to appreciate the ordinary. Sometimes it is hard to be at home, agenda-less with our kids. Especially before our children started bringing homework in the evenings, the nights were rather long. It felt like I hurried everyone home just to be bored together. In the winter months when we couldn't go outside, the struggle was real. But we got creative, playing games and having dance parties together. It's tempting to just turn on the TV and call that quality time, but if we're going to prioritize being home, we must follow through and use the time wisely. Eating dinner together only brings us closer if we work to have meaningful conversations. Being in the same house together is only communication if teens come out of their bedrooms and parents put down their phones.

Despite all the positive qualities that extracurricular activities can assist, character formation and spiritual formation happen at home. As Charles Spurgeon put it, "Take care of your character in the home. For what we are there, we really are."[14] We can send our children to etiquette classes and youth group, but our faithfulness to influence them at home will have the biggest impact. The Bible does not give specific

---

13. Martin, *Parent's Tao Te Ching*, 59.
14. Spurgeon, "Christ's People—Imitators of Him."

guidelines on how to arrange our schedules, but it does offer wisdom on being sure we do not overemphasize busyness and self-promotion over honoring him. "This is what the Lord Almighty says: 'Give careful thought to your ways . . . You expected much, but see, it turned out to be little. What you brought home, I blew away. Why?' declares the Lord Almighty. 'Because of my house, which remains a ruin, while each of you is busy with your own house.'" In these verses from Haggai 1:7 and 9, God instructed his people to build him a house rather than focusing on their own success, their own earthly dwellings. Today, we know we are God's temple. Remembering that God dwells inside our children encourages me to prioritize their internal growth rather than worrying about their accomplishments and talents. Rather than building a glass house of accomplishments others can gaze upon, we need to build homes that privately see to our own responsibilities, our children's spiritual formation being the top priority.

Busyness is something that, although stress-inducing, can also become an addiction. Even though I prioritize downtime, when we find ourselves busier, for example, during the holiday season (which also coincides with the end of the semester for college professors) and there are extra parties, activities, and programs, I adjust to the hectic schedule. Then I find myself having to readjust when things go back to normal. In a way, I even miss the fuller schedule at first because things feel a little uneventful without them. Being busy due to sporadic seasons of eventfulness is sometimes unavoidable, but it takes purposefulness on our part not to let ourselves become addicted to the busyness. Brené Brown explains how busyness can become a coping strategy. "One of the most universal numbing strategies is what I call *crazy-busy* . . . We are a culture of people who've bought into the idea that if we stay busy enough, the truth of our lives won't catch up with us."[15] If we feel the need to keep our family constantly busy, it may be worth asking why. Are we trying to imitate other families? Are we worried our kids won't be special if they are not involved? Are we exhausted from work and needing activities to keep our kids occupied? Sometimes we need to implement new rhythms into our family to help our children with obedience, creativity, or stillness. These new rhythms or expectations can be

---

15. Brown, *Daring Greatly*, 137.

hard to establish or reestablish. However, busyness that avoids a family dynamic that needs to be changed will not eliminate the problem. The problem will resurface during the limited family time we have, leaving us feeling unequipped to address it.

In thinking about how busyness affects us now as a family of six, I am not the only one who struggles with returning to margin in our schedule after it has been filled. I have found that after a busy weekend, my children struggle more with obedience and fighting. Part of it is tiredness, but it is also the discontentment of no longer being constantly entertained. Overall, my children are more peaceful and well-behaved when they are not overscheduled, and I bet yours are too. We are modeling for our children what is normal and what is desirable. Schedules are supposed to be subject to their creators, but all too often we become slaves to a schedule that we created but then feel overwhelmed by and unable to redirect. I struggle with gaining affirmation from my accomplishments and involvement, so I must be purposeful not to pass this misguided sense of identity on to my children. Part of my goal as a parent is to teach my children that our family is not defined by the institutions, organizations, and activities we are involved with. To be honest, I need to tell myself this more than my kids. Paul encouraged us, "Do not conform to the pattern of this world, but be transformed by the renewing of your mind" (Romans 12:2). Resisting the cultural norm of being busy and rethinking how we define value and purpose is a way that we can practice sufficiency in Christ rather than defaulting to what is socially sanctioned.

I can remember a specific time in my life when promoting busyness in my family's life reaped consequences. I was pregnant with my second child and desperately wanted to make the most of our time with our only child, soon to become our oldest. I planned a variety of outings ranging from things like visiting the zoo to a berry patch, as well as scheduling a weekend babymoon for me and Ben. I also wanted to squeeze in a trip to see my parents in Kansas City and do some fun things up there before the baby came. My oldest had just turned two, so I wasn't overbooking us with activities solely for her, but I was filling up our schedule with family enrichment that I was worried would be pushed to the back burner with a new baby. In KC, we went to a Royals baseball game. What I haven't mentioned is that I was two weeks away from my due date. I had been late with my first so assumed I was still good on time. What I hadn't factored in was all the extra exercising I had been doing with all our activities (as well as the fact that siblings don't always follow the same delivery schedule). For the baseball game, it turned out we had to walk a long distance in the packed parking lot and then hike up to the nosebleed seats in the stadium. I kept saying (and thinking) I was fine. But later that night at my parents' house, I couldn't deny the twinge in my stomach that grew into waves as my contractions began and progressed. We relied on GPS to guide us to the hospital with a medical team I had never seen before, and I had our baby there, two weeks early. A nurse who had believed I was overreacting and that I had ample time before the baby would be born actually ran out of the room as I delivered, yelling, "Wait!" There was no one in the room except for Ben and me, and we looked at each other dumbfounded as he picked up our sweet little baby from the hospital bed and held her until a doctor and medical team rushed in.

God showed his providence and provided for us beautifully in our unexpected delivery in KC. Our baby was small, under five pounds and struggling with low blood sugar, so she was admitted into the NICU where she received care and donor breast milk until my milk came in. My mom watched our oldest and had everything prepared for us as we came back to my parents' house, and I recuperated for several days before we made the trip back home. But there was also something lost in not being able to deliver with my doctor and in not bringing our baby to our home after leaving the hospital. This somewhat crazy delivery experience has helped me realize the need for not pushing or overcommitting myself and my family. My desire to create the perfect experiences and schedule desensitized me to my body's signs that I needed to rest and stay close to home. Just like I was not able to accurately assess my body's signs about how close to delivery I actually was, our kids cannot always accurately assess how a hectic schedule is impacting them. But it is. It may come out in tantrums, tiredness, or an inability to know how to spend free time when they finally have it. We can help them by implementing healthy rhythms that honor our bodies and our mental health.

The Working Homemaker

After our second was born, we embraced a purposefully slow pace. It was summertime, so classes were out for Ben and me (he is also an educator). Though the unhurriedness was necessary, it was also hard at times, especially after having been so busy. You may remember your own early days of baby bliss and relate to the exhaustion from lack of sleep but also the challenge of accepting another day of little to no plans. I remember many a summer night just sitting on the back porch watching our daughter swim in the kiddie pool while my new baby laid on my lap. I am not suggesting that our lives be as unscheduled as they are those first few weeks or months of having a new baby, but I do think the comparison of moving from a busy to less busy schedule is highlighted in my experience of overdoing it before my unexpected delivery and then having to reboot and adjust to a purposefully peaceful schedule the rest of the summer. It would have been less jolting to adjust to the necessary schedule of becoming a family of four with a newborn if I had not overscheduled our time leading up to the transition.

Part of homemaking is saying no to things that take our family's time and desires away from the home. Our homes should be places where life happens together, not just where we sleep and change before doing life separately elsewhere. I do not have all the answers regarding how to balance giving our children opportunities and experiences while not becoming a slave to the idols of busyness or talents. I admit that my children are not yet teenagers, and I have much to learn. I'm going to give you some of my suggestions of what I have found useful in our home. They are likely not radically new ideas, but sometimes it's helpful to hear what works for others as a springboard for figuring out what will work for us. I remember watching a friend of mine take out a microfiber cleaning cloth he kept in his wallet to clean his glasses with. Now, I knew not to clean my lenses with a paper towel or anything like that, but I had never allocated special cloths to clean my glasses with and instead often used my shirt, maybe a burp cloth (at least mostly clean), or anything else within reach. And my lenses were, consequently, quite scratched. So, when I got a new pair of glasses, I determined to try his method, and I put the microfiber cloths in a few places and resolved only to use them. I'm a few years in, and my lenses have held up great. It was far from rocket science to make the change, but it took an awareness of how somebody else did it to inspire me. These suggestions may need to be modified, taken with a grain of salt, or completely ignored depending on your family's needs and desires. But perhaps something can be the microfiber cloth for you, the small alteration that will yield results.

- Don't feel the need to begin activities too early. The American Academy of Pediatrics does not recommend organized sports for children until age six.[16] The exception in our family has been letting the youngest start earlier if the activity happens at the same time as his older siblings' activity. This keeps him entertained while he's waiting.
- Capitalize on activities offered through the school or church. Your kids are there anyway. Some of the things happen during the school day, and even if they happen afterward, it eliminates the commute of driving them somewhere else. Most schools offer choir, band, drama, sports, as well as a variety of clubs. Churches may have service and worship opportunities.
- Let kids take a break from an activity. They are more likely to appreciate and enjoy something if they have time to miss it.
- Regarding church programing, prioritize involvement when your whole family can be there, such as Sunday morning, rather than additional nights only for the kids.
- Choose activities multiple siblings can do together or at the same time. This can help them bond and will reduce the hecticness of going to separate activities for everyone.
- Limit the number of activities kids are involved with at one time. (I recommend no more than one physical activity and fine art at a time.)
- Prioritize times of the year that are better for busyness. For example, there is so much that happens around the holidays; not having a schedule already filled allows for spontaneous or one-time possibilities. I guard our evenings during the school year, but since I am home with the kids during the summertime, I allow our schedule to be fuller because it does not come at the expense of our family time.

16. Healthline, "Should Toddlers Play Sports?"

- Don't feel like you must make everything fair. All your children do not always need the same number of activities. There may be times it is uneven based on their ages, what is offered, or what they are interested in, but it will likely balance out eventually. Also, some kids are more social or ambitious and want to be involved more than others.

- Use the commute time you have together driving. Turn off the music and hold purposeful conversations with your children. They will probably say nothing happened at school and ask you to turn the radio back on. Don't do it—at least not all the time. Instead, ask specific questions and tell them about your day too. Try singing or playing games together.

- Choose activities you can sometimes experience with your child. (Coach the soccer team, play the piano for the Christmas program, volunteer at VBS, or pick up trash with the club.)

One other way to reject busyness is to honor the Sabbath at home. Though God did not need to rest, he set aside the seventh day as a day of rest to model to us the benefit of ceasing from work and activity. People recognize the Sabbath in a variety of ways. Many call Sunday the "modern Sabbath," but at my house, Sunday is not a very restful day. Getting to church, socializing, and serving makes for a beautiful but not overly restful day of worship. For us, Saturday, which is the original Sabbath, is the day of rest. My family does not practice this in a legalistic way in which we do no work or activities at all, but it is a day in which I prioritize staying home and avoid doing employment related duties. I usually do some housework such as laundry, cleaning, and meal prepping, but am not rushed and even enjoy the change in my schedule and the way that these homemaking activities connect me to my family and my service to them. When I try to jam these tasks into an already busy week, it seldom goes well. On the Sabbath, we also prioritize family time such as devotionals and read-alouds. I avoid shopping or even pursing commerce-based entertainment, which means our family instead spends time together in simple and creative ways like doing crafts, going to parks, or taking walks. It is also the day we tend to invite company over to share a meal. It is the one day a week where we often go nowhere and simply stay home. There are seasons where there may be a sports game or something else that comes up, but overall it is a sacred day to orient ourselves toward the Lord and to be together with each other at home. We do not commit to any extracurricular that requires Saturday lessons or an extended commitment on Saturdays. After a busy week, the Sabbath is something we look forward to. The Lord especially instructed that the Sabbath to be observed when life is full: "even during the plowing season and harvest you must rest" (Exodus 34:21). If we initiate a Sabbath because we know we need a reprieve from the busyness, it can allow us to begin a new week with energy. I have heard of a variety of ways people build a Sabbath into their schedule. If a day of rest for spiritual and family rejuvenation appeals to you, I encourage you to pray about what new rhythms you could establish into your weekly routine.

Although scheduled activities tend to eat up the bulk of family time, this can also happen through the habitual though unplanned things that make their way into our calendar. Case in point: birthday parties. My kids get invited to a lot of parties (they go to schools where common courtesy requires everyone be invited to avoid hurt feelings). The problem is that the invites are usually just for one child, and between all four of our kids' invites, the time commitment adds up. So, we decline often. If the party is for a good friend, we let them go, but otherwise we usually forego. The same is true for playdates or community events that include or appeal to only one or even a couple. Recognizing the age-appropriate need for socialization has also helped me. When children are young, their primary attachment is, and should be, to their parents. A study from Stanford School of Medicine discovered that children aged twelve and below are so attuned to their mother's voice that they can usually identify it from other voices. I find it amazing that just hearing our voices causes our children to feel safe. As researchers have put it, there is "profound influence that mother's voice has on children's cognitive, emotional, and social function."[17] Our voice does not need to be the only voice that our children hear, but they do need to spend ample time with us to hear us speak life-giving words to them regularly.

---

17. Abrams et al., "Neural Circuits Underlying Mother's Voice Perception," 6296.

This ability to distinguish a mother's voice from others reduces in the teenage years. Another Stanford study confirms that socialization for young children revolves around parents and caregivers, but in adolescence socialization shifts toward non-family members as preparation for independence.[18] As children mature, they become more interested in and in need of interactions with others. So, I also let my eleven-year-old accept more invites than my five-year-old because it is more developmentally appropriate. But my eleven-year-old is still more attuned to my voice than anyone else's, so I create ample time for us to spend together. I'll continue to do this even as she ages because adolescents still need to be rooted in their family and experience home as a safe haven from the stresses of managing friendships and responsibilities. Although adolescents' worlds are bigger than younger children's, Stanford still notes the importance of a family bond: "Teens' brains are more receptive to all voices—including their mothers."[19] Because of this, we mostly plan activities we can all participate in and are typically involved in groups and activities that include our entire family. Sometimes spending quality time together may require one child learning to sacrifice for the interest of a sibling, but learning to sacrifice for the people we love is a worthwhile lesson.

We can unintentionally imply that busyness is more important than well-being if we do not pay attention to our bodies and our children's and the way they respond to stress. Since I have been young, if I do not get enough sleep, I get sick. I now regularly notice a connection between stressful times of the semester and sickness. Of course, it's natural for kids to get sick; it's just part of life. But when they do get sick, allowing margin in our schedule for them to recover rather than teaching them that we should push past sickness and stick to the schedule at all costs shows our children our willingness to acknowledge our own limitations. In Marilynne Robinson's beautiful novel *Lila*, a character acknowledges, "Sleep is a mercy,"[20] and that line has stuck with me. It is easy to look at rest as laziness, but God designed us as finite beings and, in his mercy, gave us gifts of rejuvenation. Recently, my six-year-old

---

18 Abrams et al., "Neurodevelopmental Shift in Reward Circuity."

19. Digitale, "Teen Brain Tunes in Less to Mom's Voice."

20. Robinson, *Lila*, 238.

came down with sickness and had to miss the women's Christmas tea at our church. It was sad because the three girls were going to recite a poem and sing a song, and the trio was reduced to a duet. However, although I was disappointed for her, I also felt the Lord prodding me to model treating sickness as an opportunity to rest and slow down. The more we have going on, the more frustrating it is when plans are foiled, but I have found that when I am unwilling to stop on my own, God often steps in and stops me for my own good.

The message of this chapter is not to never let your family do anything, but instead to choose wisely and with an understanding, which you can share with your kids, of why you say yes and why you say no. Honestly evaluating our family schedule and rhythms takes courage. If we are not yet overbooked, it can be encouraging to be reminded of why to continue fighting for margin in our life. But if we are currently overbooked and our family is feeling the effect, it is not easy to change, especially if our kids enjoy what they are involved in. Yet sometimes we must make the hard choices for our kids that they may not be able to make for themselves. Being involved in too many things, even if they are good things, turns out badly. If you're trying to figure out how to cut back, taking a natural break at the end of a semester, season, or school year may help. Anytime we take something out of our life, we feel the lack unless we fill it with something else. Although the goal is helping our kids learn creativity and self-sufficiency, they may need more guidance at the beginning if they are not used to entertaining themselves at home. Yet over time, your family can develop a new rhythm that is less about performance and more about presence.

However, when our children's activities are not filling up the schedule, it can also be easy to allow ourselves to become busier with spur-of-the-moment events. (People tend to ask us to do things when they know we are not "doing anything.") Allowing for occasional spontaneity or having a hobby or commitment are not bad. But they require moderation and our being willing to say no to good things that no longer serve our family's good in excess. Where we choose to spend our time says something about our priorities, so it stands to reason that valuing homemaking requires spending plenty of time together in our home. However, being home together does not ensure families spend quality time together. Mentally checking out through technology is easiest to do when everyone is bored. But being home is the first step. So, let's normalize the unhurried schedule and instead prioritize togetherness and quality time. As Gretchen Rubin says, home is not just a physical place; it's a mindset.[21] Let's cultivate a mindset of homemaking by prioritizing our home as an inviting place for our family to gather and just be.

---

21. Rubin, "Agree, Disagree?"

5

Building Strong Bonds

> "Homemaking is the deliberate cultivation of beauty
> and productivity in family relationships"
>
> —Holly Shurter[1]

SINCE YOU'RE READING THIS book, I'm assuming that you, like me, don't want to just get by working and raising the kids. You don't just want to pay the bills and feed and clothe your family. Our goal is to cultivate a home that fosters strong family bonds. Homemaking requires a lot of physical energy to keep up with the housekeeping and organizational elements. But homemaking also requires mental and emotional energy to engage and teach our children. All parents struggle with the rigor that parenting requires. Yet working moms appear to be a group who especially feels the strain. According to recent data, "9.8 million working mothers reported experiencing burnout—almost 30% more than working fathers."[2] Though being burned out is not something to feel guilty about, we should recognize that if we are burned out, whether it's due to situations at work or home or a combination of the two, it will inhibit our ability to move beyond the logistics of running a household. Basically, we will lack the mental and emotional energy and vision to

---

1 Quoted in Savage, *Professionalizing Motherhood*, 22.
2. Tartakovsky,. "This Is How You Can Cope."

guide our children and cultivate relationships with them and to help them do the same with each other. It's been found that "burned-out parents tend to distance themselves from their kids to preserve their energy."[3] The same will likely be true regarding our relationships with our husbands. This is why it is so important to weed our schedules of unnecessary activities and commitments. If our family is overscheduled and overcommitted, getting home late most nights, we are not going to have time and stamina to do anything with our children besides give directions about what must happen: school lunches, permission slips, homework, and the list goes on. If our job is draining us of our vitality, it is not allowing our family to flourish, even if it's financially lucrative. If our home culture is overtaxing us because we are single-handedly managing all the cleaning, childcare, or chores, we also will not have the energy to deliberately cultivate the intangible. Jesus reminds us of our frailty and need to seek rejuvenation in him: "Come to me, all you who are weary and burdened, and I will give you rest" (Matthew 11:28). I believe Jesus also equips us to make good decisions for ourselves and our families to experience the rest he wants to give us. So, as I jump into what I've found helpful in building strong family bonds, I want to make it clear that I am not successful at relationship building if I am in survival mode. You've probably heard the saying, "You shouldn't preach the gospel to a starving person until you have first given him a hot meal." Our immediate needs must be met first because our physical bodies are frail and can inhibit us from concentrating on anything else. In the same way, if we do not want to just coexist with our kids and husbands but to connect meaningfully, we need to ensure that we, as the one setting the tone, are in a place where we are ready to pour out.

When we think about our relationships with our children, the things we do for them inevitably come to mind. But beyond this, we impact them through the conversations we have, the way we use our shared time to deepen our relationships, and the way our relationships are growing and changing as they age. Talking with our children is one of the best things we can do. It's surprising how little quality conversation can happen over the course of the day even when people spend it entirely together. There's a difference between taking turns talking

---

3. Abramson, "Impact of Parental Burnout."

and conversing. The first is about waiting to say what you want to say regardless of what the other person says, whereas conversing is about paying attention to what the other person is saying and responding accordingly. I can be guilty of letting my kids go off on a tangent while my mind wanders. They are usually telling me about a scenario that happened to them or perhaps a book or movie. The problem with my just responding with "uh-huh" is that I am not meaningfully interacting or learning more about them. If I am waiting for them to finish just so I can give them directions I've been waiting to deliver, I'm also not actually conversing. We must train our minds to be receptive and genuinely interested in what our kids say to converse with them. The topic itself may not interest us, but because we care about our kids, we must learn to meaningfully discuss what they care about. We can also use conversation as a way to model for them important things they should care about.

When we have good conversations with our kids, we teach them how to be good conversationalists themselves. If you have young kids, the myriad of questions can be daunting. My four-year-old (at the time I'm writing this) son talks incessantly. When I sometimes grow weary of the questions and ask him why he asks so many, he has responded several times with, "I'm just a talker." He comes by it honestly—you should meet his daddy. Though I'm less of a talker, when it's my turn to talk, I like to be listened to. Sometimes I just want to convey whatever it is I'm telling them without their questions and comments. While kids do need to learn how to wait their turn and not interrupt, if I really want to have a conversation with my kids, I should be open to allowing them to chime in. My kids love hearing stories about my childhood, things my students do, things that have happened in the news, updates on our extended family, and what happened in a book I read or show I watched. When I am a good conversationalist with my children, I am modeling ways for them to find interesting things within an ordinary day to tell me about, which will be especially important in their teen years.

Familiarity also means being okay with comfortable silence sometimes, but it shouldn't be a constant. In Sally and Clay Clarkson's book *Giving Your Words*, they talk about how to encourage a verbal family through purposeful conversation and questions. The Clarksons say, "With good questions, you're never at a loss for initiating a verbal interaction with your child."[4] Good questions are open-ended, as opposed to things that can be answered with a yes or no, but they are also multilayered. The Clarksons explain, "Just remember that your child's answer is not the end of the interaction, but the beginning. The purpose of good questions is to create an opportunity to speak into their heart and mind."[5] It can be easy to ask a question just to keep kids distracted as they answer, but genuinely caring about our children's ideas helps us know them.

Conversations that may go swimmingly with one child become more complicated when you're trying to host a group conversation or maybe have a one-on-one conversation that a sibling (or siblings) want to join. Some of you know what I'm talking about: one kid gets upset he was interrupted while another one fusses she had to wait to talk and forgot what she had to say in the meantime. Overall, having multiple children wanting to engage is a good problem to have. It requires redirecting them to remind them to take turns and show interest in the one who was talking, but it brings everyone together. On our commute home, I try to go around asking everyone how their day went. If they have nothing to report, I try a prompted question. But sometimes there just isn't much to say about the last eight hours. In these situations, bringing up a seemingly random topic or a memory can be a great way to get them talking.

Though I am thankful to spend a lot of time with my kiddos, one challenge is spending one-on-one time with each of them. They are all close in age, so most things we do together. This is largely purposeful, to help them bond with each other, but spending time with a child alone allows us to focus more directly on him or her. Each year, usually in the summer, I schedule a mommy-daughter date or mommy-son date with each of them. They get to help plan where we go and what we do, and for several hours it is just us. They look forward to it and reflect back fondly on our previous dates. Some families do these outings more frequently, and if this works for your family, it can be a great option. I go the route of trying to capitalize on time that arises as our schedule allows: one

---

4. Clarkson and Clarkson, *Giving Your Words*, 102.
5. Clarkson and Clarkson, *Giving Your Words*, 102–3.

child has a sick day, one has a late volleyball game, one is old enough to attend a mixer I'm hosting for college students, or one wants to run errands with me while the others stay home with Ben. The bigger the family, the more precious one-on-one time with parents is. I grew up as one of four kids, and it was seldom I spent time with just one parent. Because of this, the times I did stand out in my memory: Mom taking me through the shopping mall and letting me stop and say hello to a huge character dressed up like the Easter Bunny, Dad dropping me off at my early-morning job. If we see spontaneous, unanticipated, or even routine time we spend with each child as an opportunity to bond rather than just running an errand or having a recovery day, we can use the time to have conversations that may be difficult to have when siblings are around. Something as simple as stopping at the gas station for a snack or adding on a brief walk to explore the area can make the errand become special quality time.

One of the important but least enjoyable aspects of parenting is having to discipline our children. We cannot discipline them well unless we are first receptive to being refined by the Lord and in agreement with our husbands on the purpose of the discipline, which should ultimately be about their hearts more than their actions. Elisabeth Elliot wisely said, "Before parents can train their children properly, they must first discipline themselves. An orderly home and orderly habits can be accomplished only by agreeing together on these things."[6] The way we discipline our children helps build our bond with them or drive a wedge in our relationships. If we suffer from burnout, our disciplining practices will likely suffer, as we will either give into whatever is necessary to get the opposition to stop or become easily frustrated and act accordingly. A psychologist reports that "parents who indicated higher levels of burnout also indicated higher levels of coercive or punitive parenting practices."[7] Trust is a huge factor in building relationships with our kids, and we teach them what to trust or expect from us based on how we regularly respond. If we only threaten and never follow through, they learn this. If we allow them to negotiate and change a consequence, they learn this. Or, when a parent shames her children to evoke different

---

6. Elliot, *Shaping of a Christian Family*, 10.
7. Abramson, "Impact of Parental Burnout."

behavior, the kids eventually (even if it's in adulthood) learn this and how to resist the manipulation.

We typically discipline our children in the privacy of our homes, and the way we discipline our children impacts our homes and everyone in it, both the child being punished and the rest of the family. If a child is throwing a tantrum, being aggressive verbally or physically, or anything else that is disruptive to others, the challenge is always how we can effectively address that behavior while also keeping our homes as peaceful as possible for everyone else. I am not going to give specifics on the best forms of discipline. Different families use different methods due to their children's needs and what works for their family. If we ask and seek, God will equip us as parents to effectively guide and discipline our children. Proverbs reminds us, "By wisdom a house is built, and through understanding it is established; through knowledge its rooms are filled with rare and beautiful treasures" (Proverbs 24:3–4). The most beautiful and rare treasure in our homes is our families, and cultivating our relationships with our children and their character as they mature requires being willing to do the hard things.

A challenge of being a working mom is that though we can give consistent feedback and discipline when we are with our kids, for much of the day, we aren't with them. Teachers and care providers may handle behavior issues differently than we do, and our kids may also behave differently around us than they do around others. Though we can feel ineffective if our kids have meltdowns at home, it is often a sign that we have made our home a haven. As one writer puts it, "Home is the safe place, parents the safe people. They can let it all out because mom and dad, while they may get angry, will not reject or abandon them."[8] Being willing to take the slow steps to address and change behavior takes a reservoir of emotional energy, but it builds trust with our kids. When we explain to them why they are in trouble rather than just punishing them, it opens a dialogue. When we allow them to share why they are frustrated, we show them we value not just their behavior but their perspective. Some people consider homemaking a spiritual discipline, submitting to doing the mundane chores and routines cheerfully. While I agree finding holiness in folding towels and washing dirty floors is a way

---

8. Weis, "Real Reason Your Kids Act Worse."

to offer God the mundane aspects of our life for his glory, committing to disciplining and discipling our children is also a spiritual discipline within homemaking. It is much easier to ignore the slammed door or the unkind word. However, not only does this hurt our children, but it also inhibits our relationships with them from being what it should be or perhaps their relationship with a sibling from being what it ought. We know that "the Lord disciplines the one he loves, and he chastens everyone he accepts as his son" (Hebrews 12:6). This is also our example for how to treat our children. Relationship building means taking the time to do the hard work as well as engage in the fun moments. Because we are away from our children while we work, it may be tempting to avoid disciplining them, instead just enjoying the time we have together. But in the end, this will be counterproductive, leading to problems that will not allow our time together to be peaceful.

When I think about the situations that commonly cause my children to require redirection or discipline, most of it relates to their interactions with their sibling(s). The sibling dynamic is one of the most emotionally charged relationships children experience. They can go from being friends to enemies and back again in a cyclical loop that is stuck on repeat any given day. I am going to move beyond thinking about discipline to thinking about how to help our children have positive experiences with each other. Working outside the home impacts not only the amount of time we spend with our children but also the amount of time our children spend with each other. Most daycares separate children by ages, and most schools do the same. I've found downtime at home to be so important because this is also the main opportunity our kids have to spend time together. Even though my children attend a small Christian school where everyone is on the same campus and they briefly see each other at recess or lunch, this is far from quality time. Another reason to think carefully about the activities we let our children become involved with is that it takes them away from not only us but also from each other. It is important for siblings to get along so that they develop friendships. It's also a learning experience, as younger siblings have much to glean from their older siblings. Professor Laura Kramer explains that although parents teach their children formal social etiquette, "siblings are better role models of the more informal behaviors—how to act at school or on the street, or, most important, how to act cool around friends—that constitute the bulk of a child's everyday experiences."[9] Sisters and brothers teach each other life lessons and street smarts.

Although we know in theory that the sibling relationship is a beautiful thing, it's also really messy sometimes . . . literally and figuratively. Our desire for a peaceful home can feel so contradictory to the bickering that siblings inevitably instigate, participate in, or even somehow haphazardly fall into. We may have that child who seems to cause a lot of it and another who just finally caves. We all probably agree with Solomon when he wrote, "Better a dry crust with peace and quiet than a house full of feasting, with strife" (Proverb 17:1). I find it tempting to MAKE IT STOP because it's annoying and even anxiety inducing. I was not overly surprised to learn that the most common parenting concern is sibling conflict.[10] In my better moments, I recognize that we need to give our kids tools to interact in healthy ways with each other because their lives can be so enriched by each other. One of the most meaningful gifts parents can give their child is a sibling. I do not say this to guilt anyone reading who, for whatever reason, only has one child. God is sovereign in your situation and will give your child meaningful relationships. But, if you have more children and you're frustrated with how they treat each other, I encourage you to just take a minute and recognize that even though some things may need to change, you already have the building blocks for something great. God designed families as built-in support systems. "[A] brother [or sister] is born for a time of adversity" (Proverbs 17:17). Although siblings can sometimes appear to be each other's adversary, we should remind them of their purpose in each other's lives. If you only have one child and you're trying to decide if you want to have another, maybe consider that you will not always be here for your child. While there is no guarantee that siblings will grow old together, cultivating homemaking includes cultivating family bonds, and the sibling bond typically lasts longer than other influential family bonds, such as those with parents or grandparents.

---

9. Quoted in Morin, "How to Create Stronger Bonds."
10. Feinberg et al. "Siblings Are Special."

There are times when our kids need to learn how to work it out amongst themselves, problem solving and reconciliation building. Yet, there are other times when we, as the adults, need to help guide them. Even if our kids are able to interact with each other while we are at work (maybe at a sitter's, with a relative, or at an after-school program), their interactions will be different. A study, and probably power of observation, shows that a mother's presence influences the way siblings treat each other.[11] Siblings act differently when mom is around even if we are not directly interacting. (They know we have eyes in the back of our heads even when we don't seem to be watching!) If we influence our children merely by being there, what a strong influence we can have when we purposefully engage. We don't have to use every situation as a teaching moment, but when we remember that our most limited resource is time, it can help motivate us to use it wisely. Being together is not enough to create a strong bond. In fact, having a sibling does not automatically lead to good things. The research shows that good sibling relationships have lifelong benefits, but poor sibling relationships lead to immediate as well as later problems.[12] So, we must show our children the gift they have in each other. A psychologist encourages, "Every day, parents have so many opportunities to help children develop a more positive relationship with one another."[13] We are given daily chances to curate a healthy home atmosphere for our children to bond. Encouraging them to consider one another's feelings, prioritize heartfelt apologies, and find enjoyable things to do together are ways we can guide our children toward strong bonds with each other.

It's kind of odd how the people we love the most are the ones we often treat the worst. Though I can be guilty of this as well, siblings can say things to each other they would never say to anyone else. Unfiltered speech can be a sign of comfort in the relationship, but it's still hurtful. The same is true with actions. A child who would never dream of getting into a kicking fight on the couch over a hogged blanket with a classmate may readily engage in such behavior with a sister. But then again, the situation is less likely to come up with a classmate. The more time

---

11. Tsang, "Effects of Working Mothers."
12. Howe and Recchi,. "Sibling Relations"
13. Laurie Kramer, quoted in Weir, "Improving Sibling Relationships."

siblings spend together, the more opportunities there are for conflict. This then makes it tempting to keep them separated, but they need the time together to learn how to resolve the conflict. Although giving everyone their own space may keep the peace, it also reduces the intimacy. Encouraging, or even forcing, our kids to share their space is something Ben and I practice to help them do life together.

All three of our girls share a room. Our little guy is on his own, but we know families who have girls and boys share a room in the early years, and it works well for them. Television shows and even books often promote the idea of a sibling as a pest who should not be allowed in an older sibling's room. "Keep out" signs in these forms of entertainment (as well as décor you can purchase in the kids' bedroom section of a home goods store) clearly give the message that siblings are a nuisance. Yet, sharing a room leads to a plethora of conversations, albeit many of them at night when they should be asleep, which connect them. It leads to spontaneous playtime. It helps them learn how to share and respect boundaries. It even prepares them for dorm life and married life, when they will again share a room. One of our daughters began sleeping much better when she started sharing with her sister, feeling the comfort of another. American concepts of bigger and better often make us believe our kids are missing out if everyone doesn't have their own room, but when siblings are apart from each other all day and then come home only to retreat into their own rooms, already limited family time becomes even sparser. It's understandable that spaces need to be allocated for certain activities, but rather than having this space be in individual bedrooms, having a homework hub where siblings can study together or a den or playroom where they hang out or play encourages their relationship. If your house isn't set up for such shared spaces, a bedroom could even be used as a shared space (you may have one to spare if everyone doesn't have their own).

This doesn't mean that, especially as they get older, kids do not need privacy. Yet, there is a difference in giving them space based on the needs we see them portray vs. automatically creating boundaries before they show any signs of needing them. Even when they do need some alone time, this doesn't have to mean an all-or-nothing approach. For example, we as mothers may feel the need for a haven away from the chaos, but that doesn't mean we always act on this. Neither are people in the workplace always able to isolate themselves. Something we have found effective with our oldest is allowing her to stay up a half hour to read beyond when the younger ones go to bed. She still shares the room with her sisters, but the extra time up in a different room lets her know we see her maturity and gives her some privacy. She also usually wakes up earlier than her sisters and gets dressed and ready in the bathroom. Eventually, we plan to give her a room of her own (in her preteen years) and may follow suit with the others as space permits. But even when they have their own rooms, we still plan to limit the amount of time they are allowed to spend in it. We still plan to prioritize interacting in shared spaces. I am not trying to convince you to never let your children have their own room but simply encouraging you to think about when they need it and why, not rushing into it too soon. During the transition time when kids want privacy but still benefit from bonding with their sibling(s), thoughtful arrangements such as a desk that faces a wall or corner and a cloth canopy or curtain that can close around a bed can help give some autonomy.

Another important way to help siblings build bonds is by having them use their screen time together. I am a proponent of *minimal* screen time. One of the ways we promote limited screen time is by not having a television in our living room. It's downstairs in the den area, rather than being the focal point of the main gathering space. However, in moderation, screen time can be an enjoyable way to relax. Assuming we all let our kids have at least some screen time, I would encourage you not to let each child escape on his or her own device to watch something. If you have kids with big age gaps, this may not always be possible. But especially if your children (or a grouping of them) are in a similar age range, encouraging them to watch something together helps facilitate an enjoyable experience they can share together. The common experience of watching together allows them to talk about the plotline and characters or share jokes because it's something they are all familiar with. Some days are hard and filled with a lot of bickering. We experienced one of those days today, where there were time-outs and apologies and everything in between. But the day ended with everyone eating together peacefully at the dinner table and then unwinding together watching a movie on Netflix. I'm not encouraging being a couch potato. During the school year, our kids are only allowed to a watch a movie on the weekend, though during the summer, they get one movie each day. If you're letting them have some screen time anyway, you might as well use it as a way for unspoken connections to be formed. It's been so sweet to find one daughter playing with another's hair while they enjoy a show together. Sharing a recliner or couch together, they are reminded of their familiarity with each other and the gift that is.

If age ranges are too great for typical agreement on what to watch, at least finding something everyone can enjoy periodically can still have benefits. Though Ben and I don't usually watch something with the kids, we designate special movie nights, and then it becomes a bonding experience for everyone. Food is a well-known effective way to foster relationships and memories, and at our house it's all about the popcorn on movie night. If we're at our best, we don't microwave it—we get out the air popper and the stick of butter. If the only time a family is spending together is in front of the TV, this is a problem, but once in a while it can show our children that we care about them enough to watch what they care about. *Common Sense Media* says, "Research shows that watching TV and movies with your kids, also called 'co-viewing,' has a range of positive effects. It can support early literacy skills, boost empathy, and even help manage aggression after exposure to violent media."[14] I remember as a little girl going to the small town my grandparents lived in and gathering around their small TV with everyone to watch *The Lawrence Welk Show*. It is a tradition that had happened there since my dad was a boy, and it made me feel connected to my grandparents to learn what they liked and find enjoyment in it too. The ladies wore fancy ruffled dresses, and the men dressed as gentlemen, and the whole thing felt special because the TV had been turned on specifically for that reason. If your family struggles with being on screens too much, designating family or sibling movie time can be a way to regulate screen use to specific times. Rather than just saying no, you can redirect to when they can watch something. It can also help hold us accountable if we tend to have something on often. A study confirms that kids follow their parents' media habits: "Children are three times more likely to spend

---

14. Robb, "Why Watching TV."

lots of time watching TV and playing on screens if their parents do the same."[15] Of course, reading books, listening to audiobooks, and playing board or card games together are other excellent ways for families to bond by intentionally sitting down and enjoying a story or entertainment together.

Though sitting together snuggled on the couch brings families together, so does getting out and doing things. Our kids will get inundated with possible activities to be involved with (and if they're too young to know what's out there, we probably know). Margin in our schedule requires saying no to some age and grade specific activities we could chauffeur our kids to so that we can give them time to spend with each other, and oftentimes with us. It can be tricky to brainstorm things that can be done on a variety of different levels but still be enjoyed by everyone, but it is worth it. Activities like biking, swimming, roller-skating, sledding, and bowling all include a variety of ages and skill levels. While not everything we do as a family needs to be active, incorporating activity is also a built-in way to get everyone moving, which is helpful for our own well-being (and of course the kids'). It has been noted that working moms may not get enough physical activity.[16] This isn't because we don't want to be active—okay, sometimes I don't want to be active. It's often because we don't want to spend more time away from our families in addition to the time we are away at work, so we cut out a non-essential like exercise. Finding ways to be physically active with our family doesn't require breaking a sweat to be good for us and them. We tend to remember experiences connected to movement, so as we move, our kids are more likely to remember the memories they make with each other and with us.

Finding family outings that are less age specific like visiting botanical gardens, nature centers, or museums (which usually have discovery areas for younger ones as well as plenty for older ages) can help make the experience enjoyable for everyone rather than certain kids feeling like they are only doing it for their siblings' enjoyment. Siblings don't have to do everything together, but even if they split up once they arrive at the library and go to their designated areas, the shared experience of

---

15. BBC News, "Children 'Influenced by Parents.'"
16. Mailey and McAuley, "Impact of a Brief Intervention."

riding in the vehicle together and then reporting back together afterward about how they spent their time unifies them in a way that each sibling having their own playdate at a different friend's house does not. Jerry Seinfeld humorously insisted, "There is no such thing as fun for the whole family."[17] While I appreciate that he doesn't sugarcoat the challenges of family dynamics, Seinfeld's take is a little too jaded for me. There's no such thing as the entire family having fun all the time, but of course the whole family can enjoy spending time together. Psalm 133:1 says, "How good and pleasant it is when God's people live together in unity!" Many versions translate "God's people" as "brethren" and a few even translate it as "families" or "brothers and sisters." Though the idea is relevant for all who are in the family of God, it seems to me that living together in unity should be especially relevant to the members within a Christian family. If those following Christ from different homes can live together in unity, so much more should a Christ-honoring household do life together in harmony. Though much of sibling interaction happens organically at home, scheduling activities both at home and away from home that our children can participate in together helps signal to them that spending time together is a priority worth spending resources like time and money on.

The last way to help encourage family bonds is to be purposeful in our friend selections. Ben and I interact the most with other couples who have children around our kids' ages (and who have at least a couple of them). There does not have to be an exact pairing for all four of ours, but we seek out families who have children in the general ballpark of our kids' ages or, if their kids are older, teens who like to interact with younger children. Though we certainly want our kids to have intergenerational relationships, when it comes to purposeful get-togethers like inviting people over for dinner or doing an activity together, we gravitate toward families that have fellowship for our kids. This doesn't mean that we don't also have older friends whose children are grown or that Ben and I don't have men and women events we each do individually sometimes, but for the most part we interact with fellow families. Most of our family friends come from church. Our church is relatively small and has quite a few families in our stage of life. We should attend church

---

17. Original location of statement unknown.

to grow spiritually and to have opportunities to serve, so it shouldn't be all about what we get out of it. We did not choose our church based on a large children's program and budget (it has neither). But if there are no families in a similar stage of life at your church, it may be worth considering whether it is the best fit because kids need fellowship too. Of course, there are other ways to meet family friends: the neighborhood, work, school, sports, or any other activity your kids are involved with. Wherever you meet them, I would encourage you to prioritize spending purposeful time with other Christian families.

This does not mean we shouldn't spend time with non-believers and share about Jesus with them. However, during our children's formative years, it is our responsibility to nurture and protect them. Children and adolescents need to be poured into and surrounded by good influences rather than being expected to be the good influence that rubs off on others. If we want our relationships with other families to help make our relationships with our children and husbands stronger, we need to be spending time with like-minded families who encourage us, and hopefully we do the same for them. Paul encouraged the Hebrew church to engage with those who uplifted them: "And let us consider how we may spur one another on toward love and good deeds, not giving up meeting together, as some are in the habit of doing, but encouraging one another" (Hebrews 10:24–25). Many people use this verse to discuss attending church; while this is relevant, the early church consisted of home churches where families met together. Even if we are not meeting for a Bible study, prioritizing fellowship with other Christian families is a way to encourage each other spiritually.

Many working moms tend to have a minimal social life, and I wholeheartedly admit to this. According to Pew Research Center, "Most full-time working moms say they don't have enough free time for friends."[18] This is because we recognize that time with our children is a limited resource. So, when we find a fellow woman we enjoy spending time with *and* our kids and husbands also enjoy (or can learn to appreciate) her family members, it can be such a blessing. The families won't engage as a big group the entire time, but being able to check on the kids, observe how they play with others, and include them in adult

---

18. Pew Research Center, "Parenting in America."

conversation or a group game at times can help everyone to feel connected. This doesn't mean everyone has their perfect "bosom friend," as Anne of Green Gables would put it,[19] but if everyone is able to get along and enjoy themselves, this is a relationship worth pursuing.

Couples that hang out with other couples have been found to have stronger relationships than couples where the husband mostly spends time with his friends alone and the wife does the same. Knowing and enjoying our husbands' friends helps us better understand them and see how they interact with people they enjoy. Spending time socializing as a family also lets our husbands (and even kids) see us in a different light, a more fun light, than they may see when we're doing housework and errands. As one expert puts it, "When people see their partners interacting with other people, it appears to give them new perspective, like 'Look, other people like him or her, too!' . . . You see things that make you more appreciative of your partner than in the day-to-day of home life."[20] So, it's also healthy for our marriages to find other families because this allows us to enjoy time with our spouses while we socialize. Spending time as couples can also be fun and healthy, but in this stage when we have such limited time with our children and any date night requires a babysitter, socializing with other families often works best. If you're wondering how to develop such relationships, joining or starting a community group at church might work. Remember that extended family absolutely counts as friends. Maybe try committing to inviting a family over for dinner or dessert once a month or every other month. We have friends who go on weekly hikes on Sunday afternoons and invite families to join them.

It doesn't have to be fancy or formal; in fact, people will probably be more comfortable if it's not. If it's stressful to host at your home or your house isn't very big, finding a neutral place to gather like the church basement or a park pavilion can work. Applying homemaking to our relationships is less about literally hosting in our homes (though some natural hosts love having people over) and more about being hospitable through planning the gathering and sharing our time and

---

19. Montgomery, Lucy Maud. Anne of Green Gables, 58.
20. Kathleen Holtz Deal, quoted in Pelley, "Profound Importance of Having 'Couple Friends.'"

attention. Our kids will see this and learn the value and impact valuing community has on family culture. The author of the Everyday Homemaker website teaches that hospitality "becomes a natural working or extension of what we are already practicing within our own homes."[21] We cannot expect to make meaningful connections between our family and other families if we are not already treating our own family hospitably, being sensitive to their needs and willing to meet them. Families who are well connected to each other and who know how to treat each other kindly and generously will be able to extend this generosity to others. The friendships we cultivate with those outside of our family should not compete with our ties to our family but instead support them, allowing us to interact with our children and husbands in fun and interesting ways as we also connect with others.

Committing to being not only physically present but emotionally available to connect with our family may happen easily when we are at our best, but it is challenging when we are running on a less-than-ideal reserve of rest and patience. This is probably why the virtuous woman in Proverbs is so highly praised. She does all the things that need to be done (feeding, clothing, housekeeping, planning) but she also puts in the emotional labor her children require: "She speaks with wisdom, and faithful instruction is on her tongue. She watches over the affairs of her household" (Proverbs 31: 26–27). And, of course, she's holding down her paid employment at the same time. Creating a household culture that gives our children ample time to bond with their siblings, bond with us as their parents, and cultivate friendships that reinforce our family connection takes time. Solid relationships thrive on repetition as we faithfully submit to the process, believing that homemaking is way more about the precious people we do life with than the aesthetics and ambiance. I resonate with the claim, "Relationship-building and homemaking are one and the same."[22] In most ways, the relationship is the easiest to overlook because it's less tangible and quantifiable than the state of the kitchen, the schedule, or the tasks. But we didn't choose to have a family to manage the logistics. We did it for connection and cultivation, yet this is what so easily gets lost in the shuffle and busyness

---

21. Ennis and Tatlock, "Hospitality Starts with Your Family."
22. Szczygiel, "How to Foster a Faith-Filled Home."

of everyday life. Let's lean in to the conversations, the close quarters, and the communal experiences. We're not going to be perfect, but there's grace to cover our shortcomings. When we consistently commit to being home and using the time we have together to bond with our family, it will yield a positive impact.

6

Embracing the Role of Teacher in our Children's Lives

"Every home is a house of learning either for good or otherwise."
—Joseph B Wirthlin[1]

We all wear a variety of hats as mamas. Some of them are cute, and we look pretty good in them, and some of them are ill-fitting, but we wear them anyway because the dog isn't going to walk himself and a lopsided costume for the school play is better than no costume at all. One role we all have that connects to homemaking is the role of a teacher in our children's lives. I admit that since I am a teacher by occupation, in some ways this comes naturally to me. However, I am using the word *teacher* to encompass much more than academics. In fact, most of the things we teach our children move far beyond strict academics.

As I shared earlier, I agonized over my decision to be a working mom. Part of that was because I had been homeschooled and originally saw myself following in my mom's footsteps and homeschooling my children. As the path for my life became clearer and I chose to work in a capacity where homeschooling was not feasible, I found that being a teacher to my children was not something I wanted to (or should) give

---

1. Wirthlin, "Spiritually Strong Homes and Families," 70.

up. Because we invite other adults to come alongside us in teaching our children, it can sometimes be easy to lose confidence in our own role. Sure, we are the caretakers and providers, but maybe others who studied child psychology in college are better equipped to teach them. However, parenting is teaching. Though our children likely attend (or will attend) school and have various teachers pouring into their lives, we still retain the role of being a prominent teacher to our children. As Dr. James Dobson puts it, "What we need now is a double dose of confidence in our ability to raise our children properly."[2] So let's get this clear before we go any further: you can teach your children important lessons and practices, and so can I. Not because of our own strength but because of he who gives us strength and wisdom.

The most important role we have as teachers in our children's lives is teaching them to love the Lord with all their heart, soul, and strength, as we are instructed in Deuteronomy 6:4–5. We do not have to be pastors, pastors' wives, or Bible scholars to shepherd our children. Sometimes fear that we do not know enough or explanations that we are too busy with work and activities can keep us from prioritizing spiritual formation, but this is our most important charge as parents. We don't have to do it alone. Churches, Christian schools, and a community of believers are all resources, but, at the end of the day, it is not up to them. Teaching our children biblical truth is our responsibility. Our best attempts to build a life-giving home will only be truly successful if Christ is at the center of it. Psalm 127:1 tells us, "Unless the Lord builds the house, the builders labor in vain." Statistics about young people leaving Christianity are pretty scary. "15 million Americans have left Christianity in the last 10 years."[3] Put another way, a sobering study reports that "anywhere from 52 all the way up to 63% of freshmen who identify as a born-again believer after 4 years of college will completely reject their faith."[4] Many of those who do not denounce their faith still do not actively live it. "61% of today's young adults who were regular church attendees are now 'spiritually disengaged.' They are not actively attending

---

2. Dobson, *Parenting Isn't for Cowards*, 6.
3. Rinker and Jaffarian, "15 Million Americans Have Left Christianity."
4. Austin, "Why Are So Many College Students."

church, praying, or reading their Bibles."[5] Though these numbers are sobering, we should not be motivated by fear. It is God who saves; we cannot redeem our children, and their growing up in a Christian home is not a ticket into heaven. However, purposeful and rich direction that we give our children is promised to influence them: "Start children off on the way they should go, and even when they are old they will not turn from it" (Proverbs 22:6). All we can do is provide a solid foundation and an environment that regularly offers our children truth.

There often appears to be a disconnect with the teaching kids grow up with and the issues they encounter in the real world. The spiritual formation we offer our children should not be presented as isolated stories of the past, but it needs to have applicable relevance to cultural issues they will grow up to care about. How does their faith relate to poverty and racial injustice and the LGBTQ movement? Our kids need to know the theology behind their faith and how it differs from other worldviews (and even other denominations.) Our kids need to know how to defend their faith in front of a group of skeptics. Of course, all this must come at age-appropriate intervals. As our children outgrow narrative driven devotions emphasizing Bible heroes, it is important to guide them into catechisms about doctrine, to discuss how the Bible and science complement each other, and to acknowledge how Christianity has been misused for hypocritical purposes. When youth grow up being guided through how to answer the hard questions, they are more prepared to meet them in a secular context.

There is a passage of Scripture I had been unfamiliar with until recently. It is an odd story, so it tends to be overlooked, but it has great significance regarding our duty as parents to raise up our children in a godly manner. It happened after the Lord called Moses to go to Egypt and tell Pharoah to let the Israelites go but before he arrived in Egypt. The verse is Exodus 4:24. In it, God stopped Moses on his way to Egypt and was angry at him, "about to kill him" until Moses' wife Zipporah quickly intervened and circumcised their son Gershom, which appeased the Lord's displeasure. God had just called Moses to be a part of a great enterprise that would go down in history. Moses was about to do God's work in the world by leading his chosen people out of slavery

---

5. Ham, Beemer, and Hillard, *Already Gone*, 24.

toward the Promised Land. However, Moses overlooked his private and parental duty. He did not circumcise his son, despite the fact the Lord had commanded all Hebrew boys to be circumcised on the eighth day as a way to set them apart from the other nations as a distinctive people. This story shows the significance of allowing our service to the world, despite the good we may be doing, to overshadow the responsibility we have been given to disciple our own children. In thinking about our role as working mothers, this does not mean we cannot serve in a public way. After Moses' son was circumcised, Moses continued to follow God's plan for him to lead the Israelites out of Egypt. However, we, like Moses, must be sure we are being faithful to the things God has called us to in our own homes before we can effectively go out and minister to our neighbors, whoever they may be.

Though I have been connecting our public role of working outside the home to Moses' public role of leading the people, I think there are also some noteworthy connections to make with Zipporah, the wife and mother. Though her husband was the leader of their home, she was the one in this story with the spiritual insight to understand why God was displeased and the one who was willing to act, which resulted in saving her husband's life. Though we should honor our husbands and their role as protectors in our family, we are also uniquely gifted with discernment. When God guides us into knowledge regarding how to teach and disciple our children, we should act accordingly for the good of our entire family. This story also shows the negative consequences of first slacking on our parental duty to guide our children spiritually. Rather than following God's law and circumcising Gershom as an infant with sanitary instruments and in a safe place where the baby could recover in comfort and security, Zipporah had to use the flint knife they happened to have available (which may or may not have been clean) and conduct a minor surgery outside in the open air, a procedure that likely caused Gershom a fair amount of pain in the process and the recovery. Likewise, if we are not faithful to guide our children in spiritual practices and Christlikeness, there is a price our children will have to pay. It doesn't mean God will not be gracious and allow for us to begin at whatever stage we may be in, but following God's plan for us to begin guiding our children in godliness from an early age will allow them to experience less heartache as they lead a life in submission to Jesus.

A professor from Yale Divinity School conducted a study on young people who remained strong in their faith and found religious organizations do not strongly influence young people's likeliness of remaining faithful; the family does. "No other conceivable causal influence . . . comes remotely close to matching the influence of parents on the religious faith and practices of youth . . . Parents just dominate."[6] This sacred duty we have been given to teach our children the ways of truth apply to all parents, but, again, as working moms, we spend less time with our children. This means we must prioritize even more. Despite the fact there are a hundred things vying for our time and attention, we, like Mary, need to resist the distractions and sit down at Jesus' feet, bringing our children with us. Natural rhythms like listening to Christian songs on commutes, praying at mealtimes and before bed, and reading devotions and character-forming literature together can be liturgies, purposeful practices, to walk alongside our children in faith. Sarah Clarkson says, "[S]pirituality can be as natural as the air a child breathes if parents are willing to be creative, flexible, and intentional."[7] God has instructed us to regularly teach our children his commandments and principles. "Impress them on your children. Talk about them when you sit at home and when you walk along the road, when you lie down and when you get up" (Deuteronomy 6:7). The number one way we are to be teachers to our children is to teach them God's Word and his relevance in our daily lives. Any other lesson pales in comparison.

Another important way we can be teachers to our children is to help them grow relational and social skills. *Coincidental teaching*[8] is the term for guidance, specifically promoting social skills, that naturally happens in real-life settings as parents and children interact together at home. It takes a safe and intimate relationship for some of the hard lessons of social skills to be delivered and received well. We can only be receptive to learning not to stand too close to someone and breathe less than fresh breath on them if we believe the one instructing cares

---

6. Wilson, "Key to Saving Teenagers."
7. Clarkson, *Lifegiving Home*, 104.
8. Schulze, Rule, and Innocenti, "Coincidental Teaching."

about us and has our best interest at heart. Otherwise, it just feels like a criticism rather than a helpful pointer on how to make and keep friends. *Soft skills* are the non-technical skills related to getting along with others and making good decisions that will transfer to any career or situation. Many schools have developed initiatives to celebrate good character and interpersonal skills, such as monthly awards, but it is not the school's job to teach our children relational and social skills. As one parent put it, we can't "outsource" the socialization of our children. Many skills we can teach our kids simply from our interactions with them (not to interrupt, to make eye contact, or to practice empathy for others). Yet, children often act differently around their family than around others. To be able to see what our children do well and what they struggle with, we must observe them in social situations. This means inviting others into our home as well as being involved with the activities our children participate in. My goal is not to teach my children how to be popular but to teach them to express their frustrations in productive ways, to learn patience in working with others, and to cultivate genuine interest in others. What we model to our children and expect from them at home has the largest impact. If we don't practice social norms (such as manners) at home, they will probably not be able to instantly switch and start using them around others. Practically speaking, the way we interact with them at home is practice for the way they will interact with others outside of our home. For example, if we do not give them our full attention when they talk to us, they will learn that it is okay to show disinterest toward someone who is talking to them.

In a study conducted to better understand adolescents who have social anxiety, the researchers found that parents who also displayed social anxiety, parents who did not allow their kids levels of independence, and parents who showed low levels of warmth were more likely to have their children struggle in social settings.[9] We must always respond to research highlighting parental faults with wisdom because everyone, regardless of their parents, has shortcomings, and we cannot hold ourselves responsible for every struggle our children will experience. However, our kids are watching us. I like the way one researcher put it: "Knowing that children are modeling a parent's behavior can impact the

---

9. Garcia, Carlton, and Richey, "Parenting Characteristics among Adults."

way that parents react to situations and problems they may encounter."[10] If our children notice we do not try or know how to interact well with others, they will probably be less likely to value cultivating people skills. All kids are awkward sometimes. I still feel awkward in social situations sometimes. (Can I get an amen from any other introverts out there who can relate?) But when we model doing hard things for the sake of developing community and networks, our children will benefit. If we try to micromanage all our kids' interactions with others rather than letting them figure it out, they may struggle with taking the initiative themselves. Parenting warmth differs from family to family. Some of us hug and kiss a lot. Some of us don't, and that's okay, as long as we are somehow showing our kids we love them, accept them, and are committed to helping them grow as relational people. It can be easy to think that our kids will naturally learn social intelligence, but developing people skills, like most skills, requires guidance. Paul exhorted Timothy not to use youth as an excuse for uncultivated behaviors: "Don't let anyone look down on you because you are young, but set an example for the believers in speech, in conduct" (1 Timothy 4:12). We can use our time at home with our children to nurture their relational and social skills while they are young.

We can also be teachers to our children by equipping them with life skills such as learning to do household chores, maintenance, scheduling, and money budgeting. Because most kids spend a significant number of hours each week at school, some blame the lack of these practical skills on the schools. One critic complained, "Classrooms have become so focused on preparing our children academically that life skills have been put on the back burner."[11] However, I do not expect (or want) my children's schoolteacher to attempt to fit in teaching life skills on top of everything else. Their job is to educate academically, but life skills are best learned at home. Life skills are the housekeeping elements of homemaking. Yet, the more time our children spend away from home engaged in activities and commitments, the fewer opportunities they have to observe the housekeeping and home maintenance roles moms and dads regularly model. Likewise, the less time we spend at home, the

10. Melser, *Soft Skills for Kids*, xvii
11. Hamaker, "Key Life Skills."

less time we have to model such skills. One author hits the nail on the head, saying, "We don't ask them to help much around the house because the checklisted childhood leaves little time in the day for anything aside from academic and extracurricular work; thus, kids don't know how to look after their own needs, respect the needs of others, or do their fair share for the good of the whole."[12] Also, because parents have so many tasks to complete, it is easy for us to go on autopilot, finishing tasks as efficiently as possible rather than using the opportunities as teaching moments. Many things also simply happen behind the scenes, so to speak, that are not apparent to kids without purposeful teaching. For example, even if our kids grocery shop with us, they will not know our food budget or understand how our shopping is influenced by those constraints unless we bring it to their attention.

When we embrace the housekeeping side of homemaking, it is more likely that our children will willingly learn to participate. Homemaker and blogger Melissa Ringstaff explains, "[A]s the homemaker, you set the atmosphere in your home. Your attitude towards seemingly mundane tasks will influence the rest of your family and how they feel about the same things."[13] Out of all the aspects of homemaking, I admit that I struggle with housekeeping the most. Perhaps because I am an academic, I love being inside my own head, thinking about ideas and theories. I struggle with the physicality of housekeeping and maintenance as well as the redundancy of it. I have a dear friend whose happy place is chopping vegetables in her kitchen before dinner. It sounds beautiful, but I can't relate. I resonate more with the sentiment that housekeeping "is like being caught in a revolving door."[14] My creative outlets are not cooking, decorating, hosting, or plug in whatever other domestic art you will. However, my lack of natural inclination toward these does not excuse me from learning to do them well and passing the knowledge on to my children. When I help my children memorize spelling words on the ride to school each morning, I often catch them looking out the window and becoming distracted. I often remind them to "train your mind" because our minds do have to be trained to stay focused,

---

12. Lythcott-Haims, *How to Raise an Adult*, 83
13. Ringstaff, "Demonstrating the Gospel"
14. Cox, *Ladies Home Journal*.

especially when tempted with all the distractions the Ozark Mountains and Branson tourist traps have to offer on our morning commute. In a similar way, I have learned, and am continuing to learn, how to train my body and, more importantly, my spirit to the rhythms of housekeeping. One day while I was cleaning the kitchen, my little boy, who was sitting at the counter coloring, looked up and said, "Mama—you spend a lot of time in the kitchen." I had to laugh because I do indeed spend a lot of time there, despite cooking and cleaning not being my happy place. I am learning that I can model good stewardship of our home, bodies, and health by practicing housekeeping to the best of my ability. Our children will see the things we spend time doing as things we consider valuable and will likely go on to internalize those values themselves.

Homemaking, specifically housekeeping, can be an art. However, even those of us who do not have the interest or aptitude to turn mealtime into a visual and sensory celebration can still apply ourselves to doing our tasks well as unto the Lord. Meals do not have to be gourmet to be nutritious and satisfying. Simple meals are still an act of service to God and my family, and a home-cooked meal does not have to be made from scratch. We can value housekeeping even if we do not love it. Life skills can be pushed to the backburner because they are not readily perceptible to the public eye or evaluated on academic exams. However, teaching our children to be self-sufficient is the best way to equip them to have satisfying home lives themselves someday. Not only do practical skills prepare our children for life beyond our home, but they orient all of us to the dignity of work. Cooking even though we could go through a drive through allows us to practice frugality and reminds us of the appreciation we receive through doing something for ourselves. Thomas Moore said, "The ordinary arts we practice at home are of more importance to the soul than their simplicity may suggest."[15] The spiritual and relational aspects of homemaking best flourish when the physical and practical needs have been met.

Teaching our kids to cook, do laundry, or change a tire requires margin in our schedule. Teaching the range of life skills ideally involves both moms and dads. And, yes, I absolutely think boys as well as girls should be taught housekeeping basics. Teaching and letting our kids

---

15. Moore, *Care of the Soul*.

practice slows down our ability to do those tasks quickly but, in the long run, it can reduce our chores at home as our children begin to share the responsibility. The avoidance of teaching life skills and housekeeping skills shows the way that the private and the domestic have been devalued by our culture. You get more likes on social media by posting about your child's soccer team winning than posting about how you taught him to clean a toilet or open a bank account. Yet which will probably have more influence on his future? The Bible tells us, "Discipline your children, and they will give you peace; they will bring you the delights you desire" (Proverbs 29:17). The Hebrew word *yasar*, translated with the English word *discipline*, means to instruct and teach as well as to chastise.[16] Being disciplined can mean creating structure and follow-through, especially for undesirable tasks. If we teach our children discipline in doing the necessary but not always fun things, our homes will be more peaceful and so will the homes they grow up to manage. Something that we practice that has worked well amidst a busy schedule is allocating chores according to seasons. While some chores are year-round, other chores that the kids struggle to complete during the school year when they are doing homework or that I have less time to oversee during heavy grading seasons are pushed to times such as the summer or holiday breaks.

We can also be teachers to our children by purposefully passing on knowledge related to our giftings and talents. While the previous ways I've mentioned that parents should teach children (spiritual, social/emotional, and life-skills related) are universal, there are specific types of knowledge we can pass on to our children that will vary from family to family. Child psychiatrist Dr. Rosenfeld explains, "Any ritual or interest that you can share as a family establishes a sense of identity—of who you are as a family. And that will stay with your children all their lives."[17] Teaching skills or important lessons may require different methods than simply sharing a hobby. For example, I teach my girls piano, which requires structure the same way academic subjects do. We have weekly piano lessons, and I find opportunities for them to perform. Teaching our children something we want them to gain competency

---

16. Calvary Chapel of Jonesboro, "How to Get a Delightful Son."
17. Nelson, "Sharing Hobbies with Your Child."

in will not always be fun because it requires order and follow through. However, because our children have formal teachers and coaches for many areas of their life, it can be easy for them to defer to others as the authorities rather than us. We have all probably experienced our child contradicting what we said compared to what another adult has said. They automatically see us as an authority in terms of household rules but not necessarily in terms of expertise. Yet, I want to serve as a source of knowledge in certain areas for my children. Culture today (especially through media) often conveys the message that parents are clueless, can't understand their kids, and don't have anything practical to offer. Showing them ways that we are competent not just as parents but in the workforce and community related needs allows them to respect us differently. My kids also see me as an expert of sorts in writing and reading related things. Our areas of expertise will be different, but sharing these with our children and challenging them not necessarily to excel but to gain base-level knowledge deepens the ways we can interact with our children.

Sharing hobbies and building shared interests is less formal than teaching a technical skill but another great way for our kids to see us not just as parents but as competent, interesting people. It's good for them to realize that despite our love for them, we also have a life and interests beyond them. I enjoy doing low-impact workouts such as yoga, Pilates, and barre. I do these in our basement and often let and even encourage the kids to do them with me. I got my oldest her own mat recently as a gift, which she was very excited about. When we do a workout together, my kids are quick to tell me how incorrectly I sometimes do the moves compared to the instructor on the video (I like to say I'm modifying). So, I would not say they see me as an expert. But we are sharing an appreciation for the need to move our bodies. I am not working out to lose weight or to hone a beach body or even to do the moves perfectly. I'm modeling a lifestyle of wellness and movement for its own sake, and that is something that is becoming valued by all of us. Because they see me doing my workouts, my kids also like to do their own, so I will sometimes let them do Cosmic Kids Yoga or my older daughter do a (supervised) workout led by a teen with her own fitness channel. Sharing hobbies can be a great way to use family time at home together.

It can also be a way for our kids to learn to branch out. The Global Education Network explains, "Sharing hobbies with your children can help them build confidence in an environment that is safe, comfortable, and familiar."[18] Doing hobbies together can help create home routines that prevent boredom and allow for natural ways for families to interact.

Not all hobbies will be appreciated by our kids. Just as couples often have both shared interests and varied interests, it's the same with parents and children. The opposite can also be true. Our kids may have hobbies we don't love but we learn to enjoy because we love them. For Ben and me, one example is game night. For whatever reason, though we have fun when we do it, neither of us is a big game person. Board games and card games are not our go-to for relaxation or entertainment. The one exception is Mexican train dominoes. We like that one, despite the fact we may be about twenty years too young to declare a shameless love for play dominoes. Although it is not our cup of tea, we know the kids enjoy family game night and that it creates opportunities to spend time together, so we periodically commit to doing this. As any parent knows, the squabbles and tears that inevitably spring up when someone loses make it challenging to commit to game night as a young family. But it also brings us together and teaches the kids how to be gracious winners and losers (we're still working on the second one). I must admit, it's pretty adorable to hear my four-year-old yell out the card he needs when we play Zingo or see the little drawings my girls come up with when we play Pictionary. It's also interesting to notice the games some enjoy but others loathe. Regarding both board games and the plethora of hobbies out there, some children may gravitate toward something their sibling does not. If we view hobbies as possible ways to be teachers to our children but don't put pressure on ourselves (or them) to convert them to love the hobby, it can be enjoyable. These shared hobbies can also help time at home be interesting and relationship building, making it easier to say no to busyness outside the home.

However, we do not have to take on primary responsibility for passing on every skill or interest we have to our children. For example, I was a swim instructor and lifeguard in my high school and college years and planned on teaching our kids to swim. But the logistics of finding access

---

18. Global Education Network, "Incredible Benefits of Sharing a Hobby."

to a pool and giving my undivided attention to one child while the others also required supervision around the water were too complicated. There are a variety of ways we can be teachers to our children, but that doesn't mean we are obligated to teach and cultivate everything. Their own interests, our availability, and access to resources are all factors. While spiritual and emotional guidance should be a constant, teaching them specific skills or hobbies may require an age or interest window. As long as we are mindful of ways we can guide our children and be purposeful in our interactions with them, our families will flourish. The psalmist said, "Like arrows in the hands of a warrior are children born in one's youth" (Psalm 127:4). The big-picture target of aiming our children toward Jesus should not change, but the secondary details we aim them toward at various seasons of their childhood and adolescence might change.

The last way we can be teachers to our children is partnering with their schools and their teachers. Because school-age children are likely gone for seven plus hours a day at school, it can be easy to assume that once they are home, we can focus on "family stuff" and leave the academics to the school day. However, family stuff has a lot to do with academics; sometimes they are so interconnected it is difficult to separate them. Case in point: reading, specifically reading out loud. There is so much research that suggests that beginning to read to our children when they are young is one of the best things we can do for their future success. Yet reading is also an amazing bonding experience for families. The physical closeness and the shared experience of listening to the same stories cultivate relationships. It gives families memories and inside jokes. It gives bickering siblings a place to call a truce and sit together in peace. If you have not read Sarah Mackenzie's encouraging book *The Read-Aloud Family: Making Meaningful and Lasting Connections with Your Kids*, I highly recommend it. Sarah, a homeschooling mom of six, says, "I've come to understand, something that both delights and relieves me: reading aloud with our kids is indeed the best use of our time and energy as parents. It's more important than just about anything else we can do."[19] Despite the fact that Sarah's daily rhythm as a homeschooling mom looks pretty different than mine as a working mom, we're totally on the

---

19. Mackenzie, *Read-Aloud Family*, 28.

same page regarding valuing reading not just as a literacy skill but as a bonding experience. We must help our children practice their reading, not just when they are learning to read but also as they grow, and refine the art of reading aloud. We need to read to our children not just when they are too young to read themselves but always. Audiobooks are proof that even adults like to be read to. We need to model the value of reading by reading books ourselves and letting our children know what we're reading.

Out of all the school-related things we need to be willing to do with our children, nothing tops reading. If you choose good books that everyone can enjoy, reading is also one of the most enjoyable things—it's like eating desert and finding out it had kale mixed in, unbeknownst to you. I admit that it can also be blood-pressure raising if it's in the early years or you have a struggling reader, but hang in there; it will get better with consistency! Yet, even things that are so good for us can be hard to implement. Time is always the biggest hurdle. If we don't have margin in our schedules, reading is an easy thing to cut out, or maybe never to have implemented to begin with. One of the traditions that means the most to me and my children is afternoon snack and reading time. During the summer, we do it daily (or most days) and during the school year, we do it on the weekends. It consists of getting a snack, usually a juice box and goldfish crackers, choosing about three picture books, and piling onto the couch together to read. Though my oldest is outgrowing picture books, she often stills listens and hangs out in the living room even if she doesn't officially sit down with us. As everyone gets older, we will switch to chapter books. I didn't realize how meaningful this time was until one day during the school year when we had a busy weekend and missed our reading time, my son started crying in our minivan, saying he missed our reading time. It wasn't just the books and the snacks either; it was the snuggles and the purposeful pausing to spend time together. So, I made sure to do a modified reading time with him as soon as we got home. It was really his way of telling me he missed spending time together.

Although spending time together reading is good for our hearts, it is also good for our brains. However, if our brains become used to mindlessly receiving information through excessive screen time, reading appeals to us less because it requires our brain to work in more complicated ways than watching a screen requires. If allowed to choose, our kids will probably choose a screen over a book because it's the easy choice. So, we as parents must make the hard choice for them by offering them what is truly good rather than just what is enticing. Benjamin Franklin wrote, "A house is not a home unless it contains food and fire for the mind as well as the body."[20] Baby steps can change home cultures. Reading a book before bedtime each night plus reading after lunch on the weekends adds up over time. Purposing to practice reading before free time ensures that it happens rather than just fitting it in if the schedule allows. When we read to our kids often, we don't even have to be the ones to prioritize it. They will ask for reading time; they'll look forward to it.

Although reading is something universally important, schools, regardless of the teaching method or school type, may have quite different goals and expectations regarding home partnerships. If we are going to prioritize being a teacher to our children by partnering with their school, it's vitally important that we are careful in choosing the school we partner with. What is popular in education is often not the same as choosing what is best in education. Although the right school for one family may not be a good fit for another, all of us as parents need to be reflective about where our children are being educated and why. Is it the easy choice? The popular choice? Or is it a choice that aligns with our values and goals for our family?

It is difficult to help teach our children content we don't appreciate or agree with. For example, it is difficult to prioritize homework time if we don't agree with the philosophy that homework is useful. We must understand our role as parents within the school's framework and understand its significance. All schools say they want to partner with parents, but that does not always mean the same thing. Some schools simply want parents to support the school's decisions and authority. However, especially if the school is secular and the family is Christian, there may be differing values and goals, which can make a partnership difficult. In a moment of full disclosure, I am a vehement supporter of Christian education. If at all possible, I encourage choosing a school

---

20. Quoted in Sharma, *Top Inspiring Thoughts of Benjamin Franklin*.

with like-minded values and goals regarding worldview as well as content and methods. There are so many creative options for education out there when we start looking. Of course, tuition costs impact these decisions, but I would encourage you to consider prioritizing your children's educational environment above any other activity they participate in. After all, school is where kids spend most of their day, and children benefit when their learning environment is a place that aligns with their home values and a place where they are encouraged in their faith. However, God opens different doors for different families; regardless of where you decide to send your children to school, part of being a partner in our children's education is trusting our ability to make important decisions regardless of whether we are educational experts. Many education-related issues are less about the content of the subject matter and more about the politics, techniques, and worldviews attached. T. S. Eliot warns,

> Instead of congratulating ourselves on our progress, whenever the school assumes another responsibility hitherto left to parents, we might do better to admit that we have arrived at a stage of civilization at which the family is irresponsible, or incompetent, or helpless, at which parents cannot be expected to train their children properly ... and that Education must step in and make the best of a bad job.[21]

Practical things like knowing our children's weekly assignments, attending parent-teacher conferences, and participating in school functions can help us be aware of what is happening in the school. This is not the same as helicopter parenting. Our kids must be responsible for doing their own work, and if they have a conflict at school, we should encourage them to first communicate with the other person before we get involved. But our kids should know that our parenting role extends into their school life as well. Valuing our role in helping our children master concepts through practicing at home shows our concern for our children regardless of our interest in the subject matter. I admit I dread helping my kids with math homework, but it's not really about the math. It's about walking beside them through hard things. Teaching our children to do their schoolwork diligently, although all kids at least occasionally resent schoolwork, is a way to show them biblical reasons we should apply ourselves to the best

---

21. Eliot, *Notes towards the Definition of Culture*, 104.

of our abilities, "Whatever you do, work at it with all your heart, as working for the Lord" (Colossians 3:23–24). I've come to admit that this verse applies even to math.

Even more important than the academic aspect of school is purposing to be aware of what else is going on, especially if we are not able to place them in a Christian environment. Who are they making friends with and what sort of ideas are they being influenced by? Though we are not able to shield our children from everything when they are away from us, working to keep an open dialogue about what happens at school can allow us to speak wisdom into what is happening in their social relationships and the classroom content they are exposed to.

Phew!—it turns out there are many ways we can serve as our children's teachers. If I have been lax in teaching my children in any of the areas I've discussed in this chapter, and especially if I do not have a lot of confidence that we will be able to make major strides or get into a natural rhythm, it can be tempting to just throw in the towel. Of course, we aren't going to abandon caring for our children, but it may feel easier, for example, just to never start a chore schedule or a devotion routine if we can't commit to it daily or find a fun and engaging way to motivate our kids. We've all probably heard the old saying that "anything worth doing is worth doing well." Though I don't disagree, there are so many worthwhile things out there that the idea of doing them all well can be daunting. I have been more inspired by the saying "anything worth doing is worth doing poorly." It's better to brush your teeth once a day than not at all. In the same way, though I firmly believe we should strive for excellence in our parenting, not because we can achieve it but because it is one of the most important things we will ever do in this life, I also believe it is better to teach our children poorly than not to teach them at all. Jesus sees our heart, and he covers us in grace. It can be so easy to look at an imperfect attempt as a failure, but it's actually evidence of growth. With time, our failed attempts will become more successful. I was recently sick with strep throat. It was my first (and hopefully last) time having it and, let me tell you, it's no fun. I was miserable. Yet, in the midst of my inability to function normally and lead my family as I typically do, it was also encouraging to see the way that the habits we had developed carried my family through. We set aside Saturdays as our Sabbath and on that day we prioritize spiritual readings all throughout the day. So, as I sat in an armchair, hunkered down in my blanket, too pitiful to help my children with their bedtime routine, I heard my four-year-old remind everyone, "I'll choose the Bible story because it's the Sabbath and that's what we read at bedtime." His little voice speaking those words did more good for me than my antibiotics.

Peter is a prime example of someone in the Bible who tends to be remembered for his shortcomings. His failed attempt to walk on the water toward Jesus comes to mind. Yet, although he sunk when he took his eyes off Jesus, he was the only disciple to get out of the boat. He also got to experience Jesus pulling him up out of the waves and encouraging him to trust him. This is the guy Jesus selected as the rock of the church. He was far from perfect, but he was passionate and willing to try and fail. Yet he never stopped there. He was always willing to try again. God will be faithful to give us more chances if we desire to remain faithful. Peter denied Jesus three times before he was crucified. Yet, after his resurrection, Jesus gave him the opportunity to answer his question "Do you love me?" three times and then instructed him to feed his sheep (John 21:15–17). Jesus specifically gave Peter another opportunity to affirm his commitment as many times as he had denied it. In my parenting, I have been so humbled by the do-overs God has given me to lead and teach my children better than I did the time before. It doesn't erase the times I lost my temper or apathetically did the easy thing rather than the important thing, but it gives me, like Peter, the opportunity not to be defined by my mistakes but by the grace God gives us to grow more into his image.

Although our children have many teachers in their lives, we as their parents are their most important. We were their first teacher, and we are the teacher who knows them the best. Taking on the role of our children's teacher moves beyond providing for physical needs and orchestrating their schedule to focusing on their spiritual, emotional, social, and academic needs. It can be overwhelming to think about all the ways we can and should pour into them, but I find it comforting to remember that our children's learning is a process. It's easy for me to fixate on the need for mastery, but meeting them where they are and consistently allowing for practice will lead to improvement. They do not need to graduate from one skill or concept at any set time. If we are faithful to continuously model and engage, the seeds we plant will yield fruit. Many of the lessons we desire to teach our children will happen naturally if we look for opportunities. Conversations about God pop up as we explore nature and process a loved one's death. We don't have to wait for a formal devotion time. Any good teacher knows that the setting can help or hinder the learning. Much of our teaching will happen at home, so we must carve out time in our schedules to be home together. We must protect our physical and emotional energy so we can be in a place where we can engage and teach our children once we are home together after a busy day.

Some days will be better than others, and sometimes weekends work best, but the first step is mindfulness that although our home should be a place of rest, it should also be a place of learning and stimulation. As homemakers, we set the tone. Reducing distractions can help our family focus on the important lessons we're trying to teach, so turn the TV and devices off if it is not designated screen time. Offering "sneaky" opportunities for practice also helps. If we want to encourage reading, books should be accessible and abundant. If we want to teach someone how to knit, the needles and yarn will be more enticing somewhere in the living room rather than tucked away in a drawer. David O McKay said, "The home is the first and most effective place to learn the lessons of life: truth, honor, virtue, self control, the value of education, honest work, and the purpose and privilege of life."[22] We are our children's teachers, and our primary classrooms are our homes; let's use them wisely.

---

22. McKay, *Family Home Evening Manual*, iii.

7

Balancing the Extraordinary Moments with the Ordinary Ones

> "Only that travelling is good which reveals to me the value of home and enables me to better enjoy it." [1]
>
> —Henry David Thoreau

IN A BOOK ABOUT homemaking, it may seem strange to include a chapter about leaving the home, but this section is about prioritizing experiences as a family and taking trips together. Even for those of us who value being home, it is to be expected that we will also venture away, and this is healthy. The psalmist said, "The Lord will watch over your coming and going both now and forevermore" (Psalm 121:8). For our homes to be a haven and respite from the world, we must sometimes leave them to fully appreciate them. One author wrote, "The magic thing about your home is that it feels good to leave, and it feels even better to come back."[2] But the things we do outside our homes should align with all the rhythms and values we establish in our homes. Our home culture is influenced by what we do away from home. A homemaking mentality is about cultivating strong relationships and values,

1. Thoreau, "Early Spring in Massachusetts," 115.
2. Wunder, *Probability of Miracles*, 293.

which can still be done away from home if the family is together and purposeful in spending quality time together. The phrase *home away from home* is defined by *Merriam-Webster* as "a place that is as pleasant and comfortable as one's own home."[3] Not every place we spend time will be a home away from home, but we can seek out spending time in places that reflect our family values. However, many people seem to seek time away from home to make up for what does not happen at home. For working moms, this can happen because we recognize our limited family time and try to make up for it with a vacation.

It may be tempting to view the perfect vacation as something that can make up for the rest of the year. Regarding the typical way homes function, a study reveals, "60 percent of parents describe their daily lives as hectic; one in four say lack of family quality time away from chores, work, school or TV is a real problem."[4] Vacation, though not a bad thing in and of itself, can be used to make up for a year of hurriedness. "The majority of parents (65 percent) report spending more quality time with their children while on vacation."[5] The idealized, lavish yearly vacation model may have come from a harried lifestyle in which we push, push, push, rationalizing that we will get to take a vacation that will make it all worth it. We may tell ourselves, "I'll slow down on vacation." "We'll reconnect on vacation." It may also stem from an American mindset of entitlement: "I've worked hard, so I deserve a nice vacation." Commenting on the values Americans hold, *U.S. News & World Report* claims, "We value more money and more stuff . . . We are proud of being busy—it is a virtue; being idle is perceived as a vice."[6] Basically, American culture idolizes busyness, but when we buy into this, we become desperate for respite from it. Simultaneously, we also learn to overvalue things and overwork ourselves to afford them. It is somewhat ironic that parents may have to work extra to afford an elaborate vacation, but the vacation is viewed as something to make up for lack of family time. Not doing an extravagant trip in the first place would allow for more family time because there would be less need for overtime and side hustles. I

3. *Merriam-Webster.com Dictionary*, s.v. "home away from home."
4. "Visit Anaheim Study Reveals."
5. "U.S. Families Spend the Most Time."
6. Clement, "European Vacation."

want to make memories with my family, but I don't want my motivation to be fatigue, guilt for too little family time, or obligation to replicate someone else's life.

We have somehow internalized the idea that for our kids to have happy childhoods, they need to go on elaborate trips. Working moms can especially feel the need to vacation to ensure quality family time as well as recover from busyness. As one journalist put it, "Common wisdom has it that moms need vacations to recover from the exhaustion that accompanies regular life."[7] While I am in favor of taking moderate vacations, I believe that allowing ourselves to live a life that we must escape from is the opposite of healthy homemaking and the opposite of thriving. Accepting too little time with our husbands and children throughout the year because we can spend quality time during vacation robs us of the daily, weekly, and monthly ways we can connect with each other and celebrate little moments. A study found that more working Americans are using their allotted vacation days, and it also showed that when surveyed, 74 percent of Americans found taking a vacation important.[8] This willingness to step away from work and purposefully spend time with family is certainly a good thing. Taking time away from the typical routine can relieve stress, allow us to be more intentional and experience new things. Yet, this mentality can also cause us to have high expectations of what our vacations should look like.

We probably already know that trying to keep up with the Joneses is only going to lead to discontentment. However, it is always tempting to compare ourselves to other families and try to keep up. After doing some research on how much money the average American family spends on vacations each year, I came to some interesting conclusions. First the stats: "The average family of four, spends around $4,580 on a vacation annually."[9] This number is not as high as I expected it to be, considering the decadence we all know certain families experience every year. Yet, most families are not actually going backpacking across Europe or experiencing a weeklong trip to Disney World every year. It just seems that way because *someone* we know is going on an elaborate

---

7. Oppenheimer, "Real Reason Moms Need Vacations."
8. Wood, "Americans Prioritizing Travel."
9. Erb, "Real Cost of Summer Vacation."

trip every year, which they may have spent years saving up for (or may spend years paying off). Despite this, the fancy trips are the ones that stand out, causing us to think that most people are spending more than we are as well as spending more than they probably are on a yearly basis. $4,580 spent yearly for a family of four may not be decadent, but it adds up, and for many it's still beyond their budget to spend that much. Another stat: "The average American will spend a good part of their annual budget on a vacation—and many will go into debt to do so."[10] The average for a family of four equates to $6,870 for a family of six like mine. If you're well below this average, you're not alone, and you're not doing something wrong. My family of six is definitely not spending that much each year.

Transcendentalism was a literary and philosophical movement in the United States that happened in the mid-nineteenth century (around the time of the Civil War). The transcendentalists got about one thing wrong for everything they got right. But something Ralph Waldo Emerson said that has really stuck with me is that people may travel far away to find something that they really need to look within themselves for. Emerson wrote, "It is for want of self-culture that the superstition of Travelling . . . retains its fascination for all educated Americans . . . The soul is no traveller; the wise man stays at home."[11] Basically, Emerson argued that travel has become idolized by society as a way to change one's environment to avoid looking at what the root issue or problem may be: "But the rage of travelling is itself only a symptom of a deeper unsoundness."[12] Emerson encouraged focusing on the internal state more than fixating on the distant. A good getaway won't heal a marriage if the couple isn't willing to do the hard work that happens on the dirty linoleum in the kitchen while the kids are fussing in the background. The trip of a lifetime won't magically entice a teen who has become addicted to her phone to enjoy the tangible. If you can afford to travel, it can be an amazing experience. However, we should consider our motivation, especially when desiring to travel with our family. Travel should not be a means of escaping something; if it is, the root problem will

10. Johnson, "Average Cost of a Vacation."
11. Emerson, "Self-Reliance," 250.
12. Emerson, "Self-Reliance," 250.

still be waiting for us when we return. Saint Teresa of Avila alluded to something similar when she asserted to her fellow nuns, "If we neither possess nor strive to obtain this peace at home, we shall never find it abroad."[13]

We didn't go on our first family vacation, which I define as traveling somewhere for a reason other than to visit and stay with family, until my oldest was eight. In fact, even though I would longingly look at everyone else's fun vacation pictures plastered over social media, it didn't even occur to me that such a thing could be a reality for us, largely due to the kids' ages and the rigor of my doctoral work. But once we started going on a summer trip, despite its humbleness, it feels like a ritual to be upkept with devotion. Because of this, I have had to be very careful not to fall into a mentality of expecting vacations to deliver more than they can or should. Ben and I have purposed to mostly go small and simple, but this does not keep me from moments of weakness in which I long to give my children all the big trips it appears everyone else is giving theirs.

What I am after in my family is a moderate vacation, which most years is well below the national average cost, and a fun year that is filled with plenty of small pleasures along the way. I will end the chapter talking about our modest vacations, but I want to first discuss what I believe is more important: regular fun together in our own hometown or nearby. We live in a tourist town, so there is no lack of entertainment. During the summer, I purpose to fill my weeks at home with the kids with simple experiences like visiting the fish hatchery and the nature center as well as more expensive (and less frequent) experiences like going to an amusement park, watching a film in the theater, or renting a boat and having a lake day. When my children are adults reflecting back on their childhood, I want them to remember that *we did stuff*, not just once a year when we went on vacation but as a regular rhythm that our family valued. As a professor, I am fortunate to have time off in the summertime and weekends, which many working moms don't have. But even thinking differently about vacation time by occasionally taking off a day or half-day rather than taking all vacation time at once can help families engage with each other regularly. It is not as easy to manage special outings during the school year, but I still purpose to do

---

13. Teresa of Avila, *Interior Castle*, ch. 1, sec. 16.

something fun at least once a month. Some months it happens organically, such as visiting the pumpkin patch during October. Other months there is less going on, and I must dig deeper to find something to do. But every time we invest in another experience together, I'm glad we did. Part of loving our home is loving the place it's located. It doesn't mean we have to love everything about it, but we learn to appreciate what makes our town unique and the way it serves as a landing place for our family's memories. For us, experiencing the local events helps us appreciate our hometown.

Commemorating special days can be a way to share meaningful experiences. Our family does an outing to celebrate each of our children's birthdays. We've done things as simple as bringing Chick-fil-A to a park to eat and play and as touristy as riding the Ferris wheel and go-carts. It is an experience gift, and they remember their past birthday outings so much better than any present they received. It is something that our entire family enjoys, and it is a natural way to interweave family experiences into the year. Each family has its own interests and pleasures, and whatever they are, incorporating rituals that are tied to seasons, holidays, and commemorations can become precious routines that everyone looks forward to reappearing. I know families who have a special birthday plate they get out to honor someone on their special day. Since I was a kid, my family would go to McDonald's to get shamrock shakes on St. Patrick's Day. The tradition morphed into a scenic drive as well, as it typically takes visiting several McDonald's before finding one with a working milkshake machine and mint flavoring. The shamrock shake tradition has continued, and Ben and I now treat the kids to the same green goodness I experienced as a kid every March 17th. We also give an experience gift at Christmas time, prioritizing spending time together rather than things. But creating family rituals does not have to cost money. Having a special homemade meal with special foods or visiting a cool landmark or park are fun ways to make the day unique. Some of us live in places that have more entertainment to offer than others. Certain things have become staples in many places: outdoor movies, fairs, and farmers' markets. Even a trip to a park or program hosted by the local library can add zest to the day. Living in a tourist town makes it simple for us to find things to do. Some don't have nearly the options.

But even if you live in a secluded place or a sleepy town, just be aware. Within an hour's driving distance, there are likely community events, performances, holiday celebrations, library and church hosted happenings, or whatever else fits the culture of where you live. I like looking up the local events listed on Facebook to find out what is going on, as well as checking the calendar of events on our town's website. Going out to eat or having a picnic can just be getting food or it can be an event if the family decides to dress up or center other activities around the outing, such as perhaps going on a walk or drive afterward or having a game night back at the house.

If I were to add up all the things we do in the regular course of our lives, it adds up to so much more than a vacation. I don't say this to discount vacations, but I say it to promote a societal shift that emphasizes regular fun, experiences, and togetherness as a family throughout the year rather than putting all the money and pressure toward a big vacation that will undoubtedly not be able to live up to the hype. Why wait for vacation to go fishing or bike riding? I want to be sure and note that prioritizing fun family experiences is not contradictory to believing that our kids need downtime and boredom. Planning a weekly summer outing or a monthly outing during the school year will still usually only take up a couple hours to half a day. I am not suggesting that we should be planning such things every day or, for some, even every week. The level of activity that makes the experience life-giving rather than energy-draining will vary based on personality. I'm an introvert who recharges from being home but needs to get out of the house and experience a new environment to keep from becoming restless. It makes me happy to have activities written on the calendar months in advance if possible. I write them in pencil, and things often shift, but it helps give me a vision of what I want the month or the season to look like, and it gives us all something to look forward to.

The kind of personality we have has great bearing on how we parent and what type of activities bring us joy as we spend time with our children. My parents did fewer activities with me and my siblings as we were growing up than Ben and I do with our children. Part of it may be that money was tighter for my parents, but my mom is also a homebody and always has been. For her, outings didn't sound as fun as they do to me, so we did them less frequently. However, the outings we did were fun and felt noteworthy because of their novelty. I have vivid memories of wading through a creek for what felt like miles one afternoon; I have another of going out for a rare fast-food lunch on a weekday just because. There is no magic number regarding how many experiences we need to give our children. If planning outings drains you and you do them less frequently, the ones you do will be more memorable. If you like getting out of the house and getting some external stimulation, your kids won't be able to remember all, maybe not even most, of the things you do. But they will remember the rhythm of adventure and excitement. It can be tempting to look at other parents and think that they are doing it better than us because they are doing it differently. But our God-given individuality is not something that just impacts our own personhood; it impacts the way we parent our children. Of course, there are things we can all improve on and areas in which we should stretch ourselves. But our natural interests and our own level or desire for stimulation can be a guide to how we can best lead our children into experiences that are enjoyable not just for them but for us as well.

Not only are the frequency of the family outings we desire influenced by our personalities, but so too are the things we choose to do. Since I'm a teacher, a fair amount of the experiences I expose my kids to have something educational about them—that's just kind of my thing. Some moms . . . unlike me . . . are super outdoorsy and are rejuvenated by doing sports and hiking and having lots of time in the fresh air. Exposing our kids to a variety of experiences will help them figure out what they like and make them well rounded. But the culture and flavor of each family is such a beautiful facet of having children. Children often grow up to love the things their parents love because they saw their parents come alive while doing them, and they wanted to be a part of that. So, I still take my kids outside and enjoy myself in the process, but it's when we're watching live theater or relaxing in a library while snuggled up reading a book or doing a craft (that someone else has planned and orchestrated) that I am most in my element.

Yet, as romantic as this notion of filling each month with fun may sound, helping to resist putting all your eggs in one basket, so to speak, regarding a push toward one big vacation, little things can still add up quickly. It can be downright discouraging to have found something fun and reasonable to do only to be bombarded with habitual begging from your kids who clearly want to turn the reasonable outing into a splurge. The vendors, the upgrades, whatever it might be at your particular event, all make themselves as enticing as possible. I can become frustrated with my kids for expecting so much and "ruining" our fun outing by asking for things beyond the budget. I remember taking our kids to see fireworks and becoming irritated when, rather than appreciating the snacks I'd brought from home, they wanted the snow cones being sold at a booth nearby (the little ingrates!). But the truth is they don't know our budget; all they know is they see lots of people buying things, and they want to join in. Lately I've tried to do a better job of preparing them: "Okay, guys, I'm packing snacks, so we aren't going to buy any there." Or, "If you want a souvenir, you can take your Valentine's Day gift money from Nana and Papa, but Daddy and I are buying tickets, so we're not buying extra things too." When my kids know ahead of time what to expect, they have already made their peace with it. Of course, that doesn't mean the funnel cake doesn't look good, but I try to explain to them that if we want to be able to do fun things often, we can't overspend. I want to teach my children to be good stewards of their money, and being honest with them about why are we not buying something is part of that. I've moved from saying that we don't have the money to saying that it's not how we want to spend it. I've also discovered that the expectation that any family outing must be accompanied with eating out is a *huge* money sucker. I pack lunches and dinners a lot. It gets us eating outside at parks, and it gets me buying special things from the grocery store to make the meal memorable, but it's still much more affordable than eating out.

One reason that big vacations can feel so important is due to the traditions that are established. Going to the same beach house or cabin becomes nostalgic. The emotional attachment and familiarity a family feels from visiting the same place establishes memories that can last a lifetime. Such memories are indeed blessings, and I have them of visiting the same church camp many summers in Colorado. Even today, regardless of what state I may be in, when I smell the scent of pines and see the needles lying on the ground, I imagine I've been transported back to Ponderosa Camp and that I am again a care-free teen enjoying the week

BALANCING THE EXTRAORDINARY MOMENTS

I'd been looking forward to all summer . . . okay, all year long. Yet, traditions are not something that we can only establish through traveling far away and spending lots of money. One of the traditions we began when my oldest daughter was just two years old (and my stomach was highly engorged with her little sister) was going to the blueberry patch about forty-five minutes away. It is something that my family now looks forward to every year—it's just part of summertime. The farm has tidy rows of berries and weathered picnic benches where we eat blueberry muffins from their bakery after we've finished picking. I love hearing about the predictable and quirky traditions that each family has. Sometimes it's easy to think about such "minor" experiences as settling for not doing something more extravagant, but repetition is powerful. Our kids are more likely to be impacted by simple things we do on a regular basis than elaborate things we do sporadically.

Part of the reason that we didn't attempt a family vacation until my oldest was eight was that we had been blessed with three years of winter staycations. We have family members who generously shared their leftover timeshare points—again, the perk of living in a tourist town. We still periodically plan a staycation sometime in the winter, which serves as an effective way to ward off the winter blues. A staycation—which can also go by the term *holistay*, though I don't find it very catchy—can mean a variety of things. To some, it's taking time off to stay in your own home and relax, but many people struggle with relaxing in their own homes, for obvious reasons. There's always something to do at home, and it can be difficult to completely unwind when there is a to-do list waiting. For us, a staycation is spending the night somewhere local (we always stay two nights over the weekend) and doing some fun activities. Our staycations have included simple things like having a movie night in the condo or hotel, swimming at the pool and hot tub, letting the kids use the jet tub in the room, and having one evening out doing dinner and some activity (usually something like bowling or the circus).

Even though by many standards a staycation is a low-scale experience, we all have such fond and vivid memories of them that I believe they serve the same purpose as a more elaborate vacation. We make memories, bond as a family, and get to relax. I grocery shop beforehand and buy special foods, like donuts, we only seldom let the kids eat. When we stay at a condo, I bring food we can cook in an oven, like gourmet mac and cheese and frozen pizzas. I pack veggies too—it's a staycation, not a break from reality! We hype up the weekend ahead of time, and the kids typically tell everyone about our upcoming staycation. Ben and I usually find ourselves looking forward to it about as much as they do.

If you pack a suitcase and sleep somewhere else at least one night, from a kid's perspective, it's an adventure. I have memories from my own childhood of staying at a local hotel and being thrilled by the experience. Once, I think, it was a planned staycation, and the other time it was coincidental. We had an ice storm, and my mom finally tired of having us all camped out in the living room, huddled around the wood burner. So, my parents took us to a hotel with a good generator for a night or two. Needless to say, my siblings and I were in heaven.

Yearly or occasional staycations can be a great way to create memories and avoid all the stress that comes with the planning and travel a long trip requires. I found it humorous and eye opening once to talk with a little girl whose family had recently taken a staycation. They stayed at a nice hotel in a trendy part of downtown and did some shopping and swimming. According to her, it was the most "awesome" vacation she had ever had, despite the fact her family had gone on a decently elaborate trip to the beach the year before. Kids aren't judging family vacations according to how much money we spend or how many new states they are afterward able to put a pushpin through on a travel map. They notice when we are stressed. They notice when we are irritable. If there are ways to reduce those factors, it isn't any wonder that they will gravitate toward such scenarios. What I'm learning is that there is no need to apologize for doing something fun and meaningful because it isn't something more expensive and exotic. Regardless of your budget, if it involves spending the night, it can be turned into a staycation. Go to the Best Western; go to a campground; go to the house your in-laws left vacant for the weekend. If you purpose to change the scenery, have fun, and spend quality time together, it's going to be memorable.

We are fortunate to have our close extended family (parents and siblings) live within a half-day driving distance. Because trips to see them are not overly taxing, it became important for us to carve out vacation time separately from the visits we make to see them. However,

I know that many people have family far away and most of their travel budget is used up in seeing them. Not everyone's budget allows them to travel to see extended family and then take a separate family vacation, even if it is modest. Even if funds are not overly tight, many working parents only receive limited vacation time off from work. In these situations, I would suggest trying to set aside time while you are away visiting relatives for your own family. Perhaps make a stop en route to explore a city you pass through on the way. Perhaps take an afternoon or evening to do something on your own while you stay with relatives. Before my in-laws moved closer to us, we traveled over eight hours to see them. They were gracious about doing outings with us that our kids enjoyed. When we all stayed at a cabin together, they left a day early and we stayed an extra day, spending it as a family. Though visiting relatives is not the same as planning your own family vacation, there are ways to capitalize on small portions of time to make memories with your children and husband. Also, if you solely visit relatives rather than getting away as a family, I'd encourage you to occasionally switch it up and try carving our time specifically for your nuclear family even if it's a staycation. This shows our children that intentional time with them is not an insertion in an already established plan but a priority.

Ben and I have begun committing to a yearly vacation in which we typically spend four days and three nights and in which we travel no more than four hours. (I realize that this speaks to our privilege in having a middle-class lifestyle. There are families in poverty or whose finances are committed to other things who are unable to take even modest vacations. This is why I wrote previously about staycations serving a similar purpose if a family's budget cannot allow them to travel.) We've gone to places like St. Louis, YMCA of the Ozarks in Potosi, Missouri, and Tulsa. In the future, we hope to visit places such as Lake of the Ozarks and Eureka Springs. Taking time away from our regular schedule and calling it a vacation has been a way to signal to our kids that they are important and we value spending time with them doing exciting things.

We desire to be good stewards of our finances, so we try hard not to allocate too much of our money toward this summer trip. We bargain hunt for places to stay (sometimes including complimentary meals), pack food, and choose places that often offer some free activities. One of the reasons I am so adamant about committing to doing reasonable trips that don't drain our bank account is that they come with less pressure. I realize the trip will have its ups and its downs and have lower expectations than I would have if we'd invested more. Yet, calling it a "vacation" gives the trip gravitas to our family. It keeps from downplaying its significance. This helps when my girls come home saying that so-and-so went to Disney or spent a week skiing. Our vacation was not the same, of course, but reminding them that we did take one, although we did something else, conveys the idea that families do things differently but that doesn't mean each experience isn't meaningful. When one of my daughters was in fourth grade, her teacher asked them to write about their favorite things they did over the summer shortly after they returned for the school year. She wrote about our vacation at the YMCA. It was something that stood out in her mind as a highlight of the summer. Of course, it was also very sweet when my then-five-year-old would ride her bike down the road in front of our house and scream "best day ever!" Sometimes little moments resonate big, especially for young children. But as they grow, planning some larger moments especially helps the older ones who are already becoming tempted to compare their lives with their peers.

We do, by the way, occasionally take some bigger trips. We recently drove the kids to the beach to see the ocean for the first time, and we'd like to take them to the mountains. But we aren't going to forego engaging in lots of small experiences to have a big one. And if for some reason we never make it to the places on our big-trip dream list, we still know we made plenty of good memories and had purposeful experiences in new places. It takes us longer to build up to a big trip when we keep prioritizing doing something small each summer, but I prefer to do something each year rather than do something big every five years and nothing in between as the bank account is built back up. Repetition is key with kids. I am convinced doing something each year, even if it's small, will be more memorable when they reflect back on their childhood than doing something big a few times (or often and going into debt to pay for it).

When one of my daughters was a baby and we were traveling, my mom commented that to a baby, home is being wherever her mama is. I think that continues to be true to an extent even as children age. When we travel, we as their parents continue to be our children's home by providing safety and security. So, even as we somewhat let loose and deviate from our typical schedule, vacations should affirm our regular life, not deviate from our values and interests. For a vacation to reinforce homemaking, it should magnify what happens at home: valuing togetherness and memory making, rather than introducing these as new concepts. Leigh Hunt says, "Travelling in the company of those we love is home in motion."[14] Planning a modest yearly vacation gives everyone something to look forward to and reflect upon. But I hope it also mirrors in a larger way our typical family culture of planning experiences and setting aside time to spend together. John Gates notes, "Travel does not exist without home. They are inseparably married. If we never return to the place we started, we would just be wandering, lost. Home is a reflecting surface, a place to measure our growth and enrich us after being infused with the outside world."[15] This suggests that though we should enjoy getting away, it should serve to help us better understand ourselves and our families and to return to our homes ready to embrace our lives, schedules, family rhythms, and the physical space we do them in. It's natural to sometimes feel a bit of a letdown after the excitement of a trip is over and "real life" resumes. But overall, our vacations should complement our real life. First Timothy 6:6 tells us, "But godliness with contentment is great gain." If leaving our home makes us dissatisfied with our home and homelife when we return, it may be worth considering whether our typical life is packed too full or whether we prioritize togetherness enough. Sometimes simplicity in vacations is the best way to allow for richness in intentionality the rest of the year.

    A conversation about doing vacations small and meaningfully can easily overlap into a conversation about doing our entire lives the same way. We could talk about the same sort of temptations to buy a bigger house or nicer vehicle. Our children can fall into this too, but often they are the ones to remind me of the value of smallness. One summer day a friend of mine watched the girls for me while I went in to work. The thing they loved the most was playing in a little hall closet. On our

---

14. Hunt, *Indicator*, no. 49.
15. Gates, *Destination Truth*, 255.

drive home, they talked about how cozy and fun it was to be tucked up in that tiny space. My kids seem to gravitate toward the small and snug. At our home, my oldest created her own reading area and had a season of spending ample time in it. Now, we already had a plush armchair with a light hanging over it that overlooks our open floor concept home. But instead, she chose the itty-bitty space in which she was wedged between the back of our couch and the windows. She brought her yoga mat back there and spent hours reading in a space she could not even roll over in. The other kids were more than jealous of this reading nook. If I'm not careful, I could get green with envy looking online at elaborate reading spaces including bay windows with built-in benches and floor-to-ceiling bookcases, but the truth is the thing that inspired my daughter's reading was much simpler. Even if we had an elaborate reading room, I think she'd still have gotten behind the couch because she liked to be close to the rest of the family while still having a little privacy. I have come to view that spot behind our couch as a microcosm of sorts. For me, it represents the way that smallness and simplicity can be life-giving. It frees us from high expectations and expenses and allows us to revel in the blessings that are right in front of us. Children's natural fascination with small things may be because they themselves are small, but I think it's also because it makes them feel safe. This is why we should not beat ourselves up about not doing elaborate activities or taking elaborate trips. Children naturally find the charm in simplicity, and it's something we can learn from them.

This whole idea of which places are vacation worthy and which places are not is really a matter of opinion and—okay I'll just say it—snobbery. In his beautiful book of photography *Connecting with Nature*, Kevin Pieper writes about the beauty that exists all throughout the world. The idea that some places possess natural beauty worth visiting while other places do not is an opinion largely influenced by social norms and status.

> Only we humans assign a grade on natural beauty. Alaskan mountains don't whisper, "do you see that flat, forsaken Kansas? We're much more beautiful." . . . The aesthetic competitions humans impose on nature—"this is the number one most beautiful destination in the world and over here is the tenth,"—keep us from

recognizing the intrinsic beauty in all of nature, and sometimes in each other.[16]

The idea that a vacation must involve traveling a great distance to a place that contains beauty only found in well-established destination locations glorifies jet lag and high gas bills while overlooking the fact that we are all surrounded by interesting and beautiful places near our own residences. Celebration of nature in the Bible never specifies a location but instead highlights God's grandeur throughout the expanse of the earth: "Let the heavens rejoice, let the earth be glad; let the sea resound, and all that is in it. Let the fields be jubilant, and everything in them; let all the trees of the forest sing for joy. Let all creation rejoice before the Lord, for he comes" (Psalm 96:11–13). Being adventurous doesn't only mean exploring faraway places. It can also mean acknowledging the natural beauty nearby and exploring the local culture, landscape, and history.

We live in the Ozarks, and our family does a lot to experience and appreciate the beauty of the land and the culture of this area. But it's also a typical small town in Southwest Missouri, so there's not much racial or ethnic diversity. It's important to us to expose our children to diversity and multiculturalism. Proponents of travel often talk about the need to expose children to people and new things beyond their own experiences, and I completely agree. Yet, the idea that this can only be done by taking them on transcontinental or international travel is incorrect. We have exposed our kids to some cultural variety by taking them three hours north to Kansas City or going four hours away to St. Louis. Visiting museums, taking public transportation, shopping bazars, and eating at ethnic restaurants are all practical ways for children to experience multiculturalism without having to go very far. Of course, some live in more remote areas than we do in which it's harder to get a change of scenery and lifestyle without traveling further. Yet, you can still find the closest metropolitan area rather than feeling obligated to go somewhere distant to give your children cultural experiences. These experiences will not provide the same degree of exposure as total immersion but can be a good starting place. *Travel as homemaking* is the interesting concept that when one travels with the purpose of connecting to the

---

16. Pieper, "Beauty Concept," 83.

people and customs there, it is a form of homemaking. It is also a push toward visiting new places not only to explore what is exciting and different to us but to identify what is normal, comforting, and domestic to others, reminding ourselves that a vacation spot for one will be home to someone else.[17] When we travel to expose our children to and interact with other cultures or subcultures, this can be a form of traveling as homemaking, acknowledging the homes and experiences of others.

In all honesty, vacations taken with young families are not holidays—they are trips. Traveling with young children is not relaxing and requires a good deal of work, preparing ahead of time, navigating all the details during, and unpacking and dealing with tired and grumpy littles (or not-so-littles) afterward. Even taking a staycation can be a bit exhausting because kids (okay, adults too) don't sleep well when they are excited and in a new place. We've pinched pennies by sleeping together in a room or sleeping on a hide-a-bed couch, which also leads to poor sleep. To an extent, taking trips is stressful regardless of family members' ages because there are often high expectations that go at least partially unmet compounded by the unfamiliar. These can all become compelling reasons not to do the getaway. After all, the money could be spent on house projects or shopping sprees instead. But in my experience, the memories of the inconveniences and tiredness fade while the memories about spending quality time together remain. Choosing to set aside time to focus on each other creates a family rhythm of intentionality. Investing in experiences rather than stuff teaches our children something important about what we value. I've had to learn how to strike that fine line of looking forward to a trip without setting myself up for disappointment when things are not perfect. This is another reason why planning reasonable vacations can be so helpful. Doing small getaways (be they staycations or half-a-day's-drive vacations) helps everyone learn the art of appreciating experiences for what they are and what they are not.

I tried to find some resources related to vacationing small. There are many resources out there about vacationing on a budget out of necessity, but there is very little on resisting a vacation push mentality and instead prioritizing togetherness throughout the year. On the other hand, there is a plethora of titles on how to plan the perfect trip and

---

17. Waitt and Macquarie, "Travel-as-Homemaking."

BALANCING THE EXTRAORDINARY MOMENTS

how to discover exciting places to visit. Travel books on how to make the most of visiting Disney World or Land is a genre all its own. Titles like *Take More Vacations* can help families budget, dream, and explore. These do not have to be bad things. If you are financially and emotionally able to plan and take a big vacation each year and still prioritize meaningful experiences throughout the year, then my message may not be for you. But if you are not, I'm going to go the road-less-traveled or book-less-written route and encourage you, and remind myself, that our definition of a vacation does not need to be influenced by Instagram. It doesn't need to be measured in miles. It's really about the time we spend together, not where we spend it, and the frequency in which we allow those experiences to happen. We can teach our children to value simplicity, be curious about nearby places, celebrate life as a whole rather than just push toward a big trip, and enjoy being together regardless of where we find ourselves.

8

Homemaking that Includes Extended Family

"In every conceivable manner, the family is link to our past, bridge to our future."[1]

ALEX HALEY

IT'S HARD TO THINK about homemaking without considering the homes we came from and the other homes we are welcomed into. Homemaking for our husbands and children does not exist in a vacuum. Our homes have been influenced by the homes we grew up in, and the homes we provide for our children will influence the homes they go on to have someday. Over the years, in the parenting and family books I have read, I've been surprised by how little the extended family is considered. There are entire books on how to mend poor relationships with extended family, but there isn't much discussion about how our extended families influence, or should influence, our relationships with our children and husbands. The way our nuclear family interacts with our extended family is important for everyone to consider, not just working mothers. But, as I have discussed in the other chapters, the time constraints and specific situations working creates make it especially important for

1. Haley, *Roots*.

HOMEMAKING THAT INCLUDES EXTENDED FAMILY

us as working moms to be purposeful in these relationships. Choosing to be in regular relationship with extended family allows our children to value their heritage and build some of the strongest bonds they will ever experience. Our immediate family (husband and children) is not just an isolated little unit. The truth is that our immediate family used to be a different set of people than who we now think of as fitting that term. And someday our children will grow up and likely have their own families, whom they will consider their immediate family. Making space for extended family in immediate families helps make room for us when our kids' lives branch out. It also allows for us to have a stable relationship with family even as the dynamics of our relationships with our children change as they grow and someday leave the nest.

I'll begin with the grandparents. They say that the mother-daughter relationship changes when the daughter becomes a mother. I would agree. We understand the sacrifices our mothers made in a way we could not before we experienced motherhood ourselves, and we have more in common. I now appreciate and recognize the way my mom prioritized homemaking and draw from those values in the way I strive to be a homemaker myself. Elizabeth George said, "Homemaking is a passion you can pass on from generation to generation."[2] There are many traditions and routines of homemaking I have inherited from my parents. In watching my parents in their current stage of life as grandparents and parents of adult children, I am also able to see my future, in a way. Someday my kids are going to venture out like I did. Yet, I'm hopeful that although they will create their own homes, they will also want to come back to ours, not just when they need something or out of obligation but because they value our relationship. I try to model a good relationship with my parents not just because I enjoy them (which I do) but also because I want my kids to have an example of the kind of relationship we can have once they are adults. I am not pouring all this time and energy into parenting them well just to assume we will lose contact once they turn eighteen!

There is an old parable about a father and son who are traveling with a grandfather who is to be taken far away to a care facility. The adult son does not show much concern for his aging father, though he

---

2. Original location of statement unknown.

shows interest in his son. Near the end of the journey, the son tells his father he has been paying close attention to the path they have taken. The father asks why, and the son responds so that he will know where to take him someday. I am not using this parable to make an argument for or against nursing homes, as there are variety of situations and reasons (good and bad) people use these. This parable highlights that the way we treat our adult parents and the way we value or devalue or relationships with them teaches our children important lessons about the worth of their future relationships with us. If we talk poorly about our parents or in-laws in front of our children, begrudge the time we spend with them, or avoid spending time with them, we are teaching our children that it is not worthwhile for adult children to spend time with their parents and that parents no longer have wisdom to offer their children once they become adults. Many movies show the obligatory visit to see family (usually around the holidays) as something that is unenjoyable and usually goes poorly, but these are unhealthy messages for families. In passing on these messages, young parents are shooting themselves in the foot, so to speak, regarding what they are teaching their children about their own future relationship.

Not all of us have good relationships with our families of origin; not all of us come from homes we want to imitate. If this is your story, I am not suggesting that you expose your family to toxic environments or unsafe situations, but if their influence will not be harmful, I encourage you to seek restoration with your parent(s) if they are still living. As we journey through nurturing our homes and families, we may be able to have sympathy for our parents' actions and even mistakes as we acknowledge that we too have and will continue to make mistakes as parents. No one escapes their childhood without being hurt by their parents, though much of it is unintentional. Imperfect people cannot parent perfectly. (And let's not forget, no child is perfect either.) Conflicts between parents and their adult children are common in modern American families but a psychotherapist assures "that both parents and adult children would prefer a loving, harmonious, and fulfilling relationship, and that such a relationship is possible with time."[3] If we have been blessed with good childhoods and strong bonds with our parents,

---

3. Gilbertson, *Reconnecting with Your Estranged Adult Child*, 3.

we should bring that into our current family dynamic. If we have had difficult childhoods and poor relationships with our parents, we cannot change the past, but we can work to mend the relationship and show our children the value of maintaining a relationship even into adulthood.

We may be tempted to view our household as including only our children and spouses, forgetting about the other important family bonds that have helped mold us into the people we are today. Therapist Terry Gaspard speculates that "cultural trends that emphasize individualism [and] an emphasis on personal growth"[4] can hurt the parent–adult child relationship. Honoring our adult fathers and mothers, as God commands, does not mean obedience as it did when we were young. However, honoring our parents is not only one of the Ten Commandments but it is a command Jesus specifically referenced. In fact, he pointed out his displeasure in the way that the money people should have given their parents was instead used as a tithe to the synagogue. "For God said, 'Honor your father and mother' . . . But you say that if anyone declares that what might have been used to help their father or mother is 'devoted to God,' they are not to 'honor their father or mother' with it. Thus you nullify the word of God" (Matthew 15:4–6). Of course, Jesus was not against tithing, but the bigger picture for today's context is that we should not forget our allegiance to our family for something we consider more valuable or worthwhile. While in some families money may be a needed resource, for many it's time. As working moms, time is one of our most limited resources, but it is the necessary building block for strong relationships. We can honor grandparents' contribution to our family by making time for them, valuing the sacrifices they have made and the wisdom and assistance they still have to offer. A childcare advocate explains, "The original village was grandparents when you look back historically."[5] Yet, because of the hecticness of everyday life, it can be easy to only focus on the essentials: school, work, and pre-scheduled activities. Things that are good for us but unessential to weekly maintenance can accidentally fall through the cracks. Yet, when we don't prioritize these relationships, we and our kids suffer. There's a lot of research showing that grandchildren benefit from spending time

---

4. Gaspard, "How Parental Relationships Can Improve."
5. Italie, "Working Families Enlist Grandparents."

with their grandparents. Grandparents often help their grandchildren's emotional well-being and social skills as well as help parents with caring for the children. They also help provide stability and wisdom.[6] Margaret Mead went so far as to say, "Everyone needs to have access both to grandparents and grandchildren in order to be a full human being."[7]

There are many benefits to prioritizing a relationship with grandparents, but when we do not live close by, this becomes more difficult. Although many people still live near their hometown and parents, those of us with careers that required years of training are more likely to live further away. (I'm included in this group though I'm much closer to my family than some.) One study reports, "Those with college and professional degrees are much more likely to live farther from their parents . . . especially if spouses are juggling the career aspirations of two professionals."[8] The likelihood of living further from parents increases if your work is something you consider not just a job but a career. A historian noted, "[I]n recent decades the majority of American families have experienced weakening [extended] family ties and high rates of mobility and dispersion. I would argue that these factors have made the opportunities for familial alienation greater than in the past."[9] What I have found is the further we live from our family, the easier it is to avoid tiffs that inevitably happen when interacting regularly and intimately but the harder it is to cultivate deep relationships because it often feels like we are just trying to catch up. Whether you live some distance from your parents/in-laws or it's just the busyness of life that makes it difficult to spend quality time together, I encourage you to consider how you can prioritize their role in your life. Proverbs 17:6 tells us, "Children's children are a crown to the aged, and parents are the pride of their children."

It's a little over a three-hour drive from where we live in Branson to where my parents live in Kansas City. Over the seventeen years we have lived in the Ozarks, Ben and I have considered moving closer, as all of my siblings live or have at one point lived there as well. Yet, we have found that we enjoy the small-town feel of Branson over the big-city

---

6. Yorgason and Gustafson, "Linking Grandparent Involvement."
7. Mead, *Blackberry Winter*.
8. Bui and Miller, "Typical American."
9. Coleman, "Shift in American Family Values."

vibe of KC. We have also found that living in Branson is better for our own nuclear family because commutes are shorter, the cost of living is lower, and we have many precious friend circles in Branson through our church, jobs, and community. I used to carry some guilt about not living closer to my family. (I know, I know—it's just a stone's throw away compared to the distance many endure, but it's far enough to miss doing life together on a regular basis.) Yet, I have come to realize that my priority needs to be our family of six and what is best for us. We're happy and supported where we live. But this also means I am very purposeful in seeing my family to make sure our bond is strong and my kids grow up with ample memories of the role of their extended family in their lives. When you ask my kids about their favorite place in the world (aside from home), they usually say KC. My mom is a natural homemaker. Her home is filled with the smell of vanilla candles and chili or tacos warming on the stove. It's important to her that every grandchild has a cozy place to sleep and that her hallway proudly displays as many family photos as she can squeeze in. My dad is always busy doing something outside, and it feels natural for the kids and Ben to jump in and join whatever is going on. We probably make it up to KC about seven times a year. It's easier during the summertime, but during the school year squeezing in weekend trips is challenging. Yet, we make it happen because we know it's worth it. The trips keep us close and model to my kids that we prioritize seeing our family. We make it for the big things like holidays but also try to make it just because. I don't want my kids to learn that the only times families see each other are holidays. Not everyone gets to visit their childhood home, but my parents still live in the house we moved into when I was ten. Going home often grounds me, and it reminds me of the things that were important in my childhood that I want to pass on to my children. It wasn't vacations and name-brand clothing. It was praying together at bedtime and cheering on each other at soccer games. It was riding the go-cart in the backyard on long summer afternoons and going to church together as a family.

For working moms, relationships with grandparents are also important for practical reasons. The childcare dynamic comes up for many dual-working families. "2 in 5 working parents (42%) rely on grandmothers for childcare."[10] Of course, this is only an option for those who live close to their relatives. However, occasional babysitting is still common for families more spread out. While I have never had a family member watch our children full-time, my mom has watched the kids up to a week at a time at her home and has also come to ours to fill in for several days while I have been away on a work trip. Although Ben is always still there, she is a huge help in dropping off and picking up the kids from school, managing meals, and keeping their minds off things while I'm away. My in-laws, who are about forty-five minutes away, also sometimes babysit if we need someone to fill in for a day or even for a weekend getaway.

While having grandparents who can help babysit is a blessing, part of purposefully maintaining a thriving atmosphere in our home and with our loved ones is making sure that the interactions are healthy for everyone. Just as it's not healthy for mama to do all the housework and become burned out and bitter, it's not healthy to expect or let grandparents (usually grandmas) take on a larger caregiving role than they can sustain. Finding the balance where grandparents are shown they are needed and wanted but not obligated can help maintain a good relationship. One anonymous grandparent candidly shared some of the challenges of watching grandchildren full-time: "Sometimes I resent the fact that I don't get to just be their grandmother, the kind that bakes cookies with them and gets to spoil them, then sends them home. I love keeping them, but I wonder how their feelings about me will be in the future. Will this make them closer to me, or will I always be 'the baby sitter'?"[11] Appreciation can go a long way, as many grandparents provide free childcare. Reevaluating the arrangement as children grow or more are added to the family can be a good idea so grandparents don't feel stuck in an arrangement that no longer works. Sometimes childcare can hurt a relationship if childcare is the only reason grandparents are included. If we only call to ask them to babysit rather than to come for a visit or do something together, they might feel used.

Whether grandparents watch their grandchildren full-time or occasionally, tension can also form through conflicts about child-rearing

---

10. Harris Poll, "Are Grandmothers Who Provide Childcare Key?"
11. Gardner, "Grandmothers Weigh In."

regarding issues such as diet, screen time, and discipline. Child-rearing speaks deeply about a person's priorities and values, so it is only natural that disagreement over the right way to do something can be personal. Some of these tensions feel especially strong for women, who tend to do the bulk of the child-rearing. For mothers and daughters, when a daughter raises her children differently than she was raised or requests not to have her children cared for in a way that she was, it is only natural for grandma to feel some hurt or become offended. While parents pay daycare facilities to care for their children and then feel justified in complaining if there is a problem, the situation is much different when a grandparent comes into our home or our children go into theirs. It can be helpful to keep in mind the value of both relationships—that with our parents or in-laws as well as our children (and our duty to make decisions for their well-being). Some things are worth letting slide for the sake of the relationship while other things that are fundamental to our convictions about how to feed or discipline our children may be worth discussing, even if it is uncomfortable.

The parent-child relationship is dynamic, ever changing as time marches on. Right now we are in the middle—the connector to our children and their grandparents. Someday we will likely be the one on the edge, as our own children become the bridge to us and our grandchildren. I try to remember that homemaking is not just about my little family of six. One mother wisely wrote, "Homemaking is about celebrating each other, and about caring for each other, as well as for your friends and extended families and even the occasional stranger."[12] If your relationship with the grandparents is a little tense, that doesn't make it easy to receive criticism about your parenting choices, especially from a family member. However, we can be confident in our choices while still being open to wisdom gained through experience. I have come to realize that a lot of parenting boils down to personality and preference. For example, I grew up in a home with a high level of order because my mom thrives on structure. I also need a degree of order, but not to the same level. Because of this, I raise my children in a house a little less tidy and organized. My kids abuse our furniture more than I'd like to admit, and their toys are considered picked up if they are put in a bin unsorted.

---

12. Holly Schurter, quoted in Savage, *Professionalizing Motherhood*, 22.

Yet, my kids need to learn to respect the rules at Nana's. When she tells them to do or not do something when we visit that I don't have a problem with, I tell them, "Nana's house, Nana's rules." Creating a hierarchy about something that comes down to personality and the dynamic of each individual family doesn't help anyone. We all have our preferences and our quirks. Our kids' teachers or caregivers have them too, but the closer the relationship, the more obvious they become.

Not only is the relationship with grandparents one worth prioritizing, but so are ones with siblings. Some of the sweetest fruits of homemaking are cultivating our kids as individuals and strengthening their bond with us and each other (if you have multiple children). I try to be conscientious about helping my children build bonds with each other because one of the greatest gifts in my life is my siblings. We grew up close, and we are still close today. Just as I talked about modeling the sort of relationships we want to have with our children someday through our relationships with our parents, I also try to model the sort of relationships they can have with each other someday by the way they see me interact with my two sisters and my brother. Because we grew up in the same home, despite our differences, there are similar values and visions we share for our families. I know this is not the case for everyone. Some people have very complicated relationships with their siblings. They are not always safe and enjoyable people to be around. However, there is an amazing tie we share with those we are bound to by blood. Shared history and genetics go a long way, despite the extremely different ways siblings can remember our childhoods and despite the very different personalities and interests we may have. One scholar reports that sibling relationships are "among the more resilient, long lasting, and intimate of family ties, and with the introduction of children, the roles of aunt and uncle are added to the mix of bonds linking siblings and their partners of spouses."[13] Even if your relationship with your sibling(s) is hard and less than you hoped for, I encourage you to not give up on it.

Having close relationships with our siblings is proven to increase our quality of life. A researcher who studies sibling relationships reported that those with good sibling relationships throughout their life experienced better mental and psychological health as well as social

---

13. Milardo, *Forgotten Kin*, 1.

relationships.[14] Now I'm going to talk a little bit specifically about the sister relationship. As siblings age, this is the relationship that tends to be the strongest, probably because women are relational beings. (If you have a sister-in-law, this relationship can also be quite strong.) A term in African American culture for women who help raise their children together, acting as mentors, assistors, and peers, is *othermothers*.[15] These women can be relatives of any sort as well as non-family-members. Thinking about our role as homemakers, sisters can be othermothers who support one another in the practical and the philosophical aspects of parenting. We must be protective about who we invite into our home and whose homes we entrust our children to go into, but in healthy adult sibling relationships, visits to or from aunts and uncles (and their progeny) can be encouraging and fun (as well as, very likely, chaotic). Teaching our children the value of family and allowing their lives to be enriched by extended family members is something that women do more naturally than men. One scholar called women *kin keepers*, "key figures in the development and routine maintenance of family relationships within and across households."[16] Despite the importance of our individual households, prioritizing ways that each household intersects with other households gives our children more role models and gives us the network we need to have and to be for someone else.

Some of the most beautiful relationships in the Bible are between siblings: Miriam helped rescue Moses, and Aaron stood by Moses' side and helped him lead the Jews out of Egypt. Several stories are about difficult sibling relationships that God restored: Esau forgave Jacob for securing his birthright and wept and embraced him at their reunion; Joseph chose to forgive his brothers and save them from famine. In the New Testament, Mary, Martha, and Lazarus all followed Jesus together and James and John, the sons of Zebedee, served as his disciples together. All these examples from Scripture show the need for interaction in order for such relationships to be possible. Just as with parents, living far away from siblings makes connecting more difficult, but it is worth prioritizing. My sisters and I have met up to do mini family

14. Suttie, "How Your Siblings Can Make You Happier."
15. Collins, "The Meaning of Motherhood in Black Culture," 46–47.
16. Milardo, *Forgotten Kin*, 9.

vacations together; as a big happy family we have holiday traditions outside of the big holidays like getting everyone together over Memorial Day weekend and at the Fourth of July. Because our extended family is so big (there are ten adults and seventeen grandchildren present on my side of the family), I also try to make time to spend with each of my sibling's families individually. Major holidays and such are fun because they are large gatherings, but it can be hard to really go deep when so much is going on.

Now a word about in-laws. I lucked out in having amazing in-laws; I get along with them well and have never felt judged or scrutinized by them. I know this is not the case for everyone. Some have very difficult in-law situations. But whether it's parents-in-law or brother(s) and sister(s)-in-law, these are also important relationships. If we only prioritize our side of the family, this sends a message to our kids, especially if we have sons. Although women more naturally reach out in relationships, including those with family, than men, I want my son to see that it's cool for men to hang out with their families of origin, not just to merge into the family they marry into. I'll admit that we do not see our in-laws as often as my side of the family and that our family culture is not always the same as our in-laws. Some of our goals as well as the specific ways we carry those out may be different. But different isn't the same as bad. Being in community with people and families who do things differently in certain ways exposes our children to the myriad of ways to do life. The hospitality of homemaking is something that relates to the way that we engage with family members. Though friends spend time in each other's home, a lot of time is also spent in third spaces like restaurants and parks, or interacting in whatever activities bring the group together. Extended families, especially as they age, probably spend more time in each other's homes than friends do. We want to create an inviting atmosphere for our own husbands and children as well as our parents and siblings. But I have found that hospitality is especially important with in-laws because everyone who lives with us or with whom we previously lived knows the "codes," but in-laws may not, and we may not know theirs, or at least didn't to begin with.

For example, at my parents' house, my mom appreciates it when everyone pitches in to help clean up after a meal, despite the fact we're bumping into each other as we maneuver fitting as many bodies as possible into the small kitchen. At my in-laws' house, they ask people to put the dishes in the sink and plan to get to them later once we leave. I often help wash them, but only under protest. Then when my parents come to visit, even when I want my mom to enjoy herself, she usually excuses herself to work in the kitchen. When my in-laws come, they help stack dishes and then give me the space they like to have in their own kitchen. Neither way is right or wrong. It is just one example of how the way that we grew up and the way we do things in our own homes influences the way we interact with our extended family. I'll give you another example, this time involving parenting. When we visit my sister, she expects her kids to eat what they have been served. When they were little, if they didn't finish their meal, she would get it back out for them to eat at the next meal. When we visit my sister in-law, she allows each child to choose for him or herself what they want to eat. I'm somewhere in the middle. I expect my kids to eat what I prepare for them but will only withhold dessert, which is typically a piece of candy or gum, if they don't finish it. As my kids watch different families navigate issues like meals, I try to explain that we do things as we do because it works for us and we believe it's beneficial for us. As parents, it can be tempting to teach our kids that the way we do things is superior to any other way, but this often isn't the case. There are multiple good ways to parent and homemake. Interacting with family, especially family that does things differently, can allow us to practice humility in saying why things work for us while not prescribing them for others. Even after years of marriage, there may be striking differences in how your husband's family does things compared to yours. Ultimately there is no longer his and hers; they are both our family, but there may be less consensus amongst in-laws about dynamics regarding hosting, levels of formality or informality, prioritizing traditions, and the list goes on.

Despite the importance of establishing rituals and rhythms with our children, it is also important to teach them flexibility, especially to allow us to engage with family who do things differently. Paul talked about "becoming all things to all people" for the sake of relationships that are God honoring (1 Corinthians 9:22). This is relevant in all relationships, but extended-family relationships are often more intense;

they involve interacting with each other for longer intervals of time than we may socialize with most friends; they may involve spending the night and feeding lots of mouths. This does not mean boundaries don't play a part; protecting and cultivating our nuclear family must be our priority. But regarding the host of minor ways families can vary, being flexible for the sake of nurturing good relationships with our in-laws can go a long way. Couples that struggle with interacting with in-laws are at a higher risk for divorce.[17] This shows that, although a man and woman start their own life when they marry, our extended families influence our family's well-being.

One beautiful result of prioritizing relationships with in-laws as well as siblings is the natural way this allows us to give our kids the gift of cousins. Watching my kids develop close friendships with their cousins only gets sweeter as they and their relationships grow. My kids have good relationships with their cousins on both sides of our family. They are close in age to the cousins on my side and a fair amount younger than their cousins on Ben's side, and both types of relationships delight them. Cousin relationships are less intense than sibling relationships but can still be very powerful. Sometimes if sibling tensions are stressed, cousin relationships can help mediate them or remind kids of the need for family. Therapist Larry Shushansky explains, "Relationships with cousins afford a certain space, a certain independence, that allows us to have different kinds of experiences with them."[18] First cousins share 12.5 percent of their DNA[19] and, of course, they also share family members. I was not able to develop a close relationship with most of my cousins, but the older I grow, the more I value those relationships for our shared history. The love that my kids have for their cousins (and vice versa) is something I honestly didn't know could exist outside of sibling relationships. Of course, there are squabbles but, overall, they intrinsically seem to know the special role their cousins have in their lives. Recently, we were able to get a photographer to take family photos of both sides of our extended family (separate shoots). It was such a sweet experience to see the cousins interact with each other. As they walked

17. Fiori et al., "You Aren't as Close."
18. Asa, "Why Cousins Matter."
19. Ram, "DNA by the Entirety."

through a field together holding hands or gathered in a cousin huddle, they were not just posing for the camera. Their fondness for each other was undeniable; it's something that has been growing since they were babies. Now when I thumb through the prints of that photo shoot, I'm not just thankful to have photogenic children and nieces and nephews (though they are all pretty darn cute); I'm thankful for this little tribe and their powerful love for each other. These feelings and commitment toward each other don't magically happen just by getting together at the holidays for a few hours. It takes consistent intentionality to build these bonds. I am excited to see the way that these experiences influence my children in the sorts of relationships they have with each other as they marry and have children of their own.

My children see the way the aunts and uncles prioritize spending time together and the way we all open our homes to each other. They see a variety of household dynamics, which exposes them to the many ways that families can function. Some of their aunts work like me and others stay home. Some cousins have never experienced daycare or babysitters while mine have. Most of their cousins are homeschooled and some attend public school, while mine attend private school. Ben leaves and works typical hours, but my children see other possibilities as one uncle works from home and often travels while two have nontraditional schedules that often include overnight shifts. We get to talk about the way that parents' work impacts family rhythms and about the myriad of ways families can mold a life that works well for their family.

The beautiful thing about thinking about homemaking as a lifestyle that prioritizes values and relationships with extended family is that it brings those loved ones into our space and also extends their space to us. My kids do not just feel at home in our home; they feel at home at their grandparents' and aunts and uncles' homes as well, and I am so grateful. James Baldwin wrote, "Perhaps home is not a place but simply an irrevocable condition."[20] There is a fair amount of speculation about what the character who said this in Baldwin's novel meant, but to me it means that the conditions for making a home a place of comfort are not exclusive to one physical place and group. When we are like-minded with others who also prioritize nurturing a healthy family environment,

---

20. Baldwin, *Giovanni's Room*, 99.

we can practice homemaking in a collective sense. Families do need to spend time on their own cultivating their own unit, but prioritizing being together as an extended family is valuable. We can tell our kids family is important, but when we live it through the way we spend our time, the message resonates deeper. An easy way to remind us of the importance of our extended family is to make sure we display pictures of them in our homes. Rather than only having pictures of our children and family strewn about us, including pictures of grandparents, cousins, and aunts and uncles can serve as a daily reminder of how valuable these relationships are and maybe even remind us to initiate spending time together, whether that's keeping in touch through a text message or phone call or getting together in person.

Making time for extended family will always require some juggling and calendar swapping. Finding time to fit in anything beyond work, kids' activities, and household upkeep is hard. There are reports noting that working women tend to suffer from loneliness.[21] We socialize less at work because we are trying to get our work finished so we can concentrate on our families at home. We also socialize less outside of work because we don't want to take the time away from our family. Yet, there is also research showing that women tend to prioritize extended family relationships,[22] which suggests that there is an odd cultural assumption that socializing with friends must be with people outside of our family, that being best friends with an unrelated person is healthy but being close with a sibling or parent is a sort of codependency. Yet, our families should be a built-in support network and friend group. Although we don't get to choose our family the way we do our friends, we do get to choose the sort of relationships we try to cultivate with them. Seeing family does not just have to be something to check off our to-do list; it can be an important way for our kids to connect with their family history. It is a way we can be blessed by meaningful friendships that enrich our lives. An old Spanish proverb says, "An ounce of blood is worth more than a pound of friendship." I do not have the authority to flout a proverb, but this idea that it's either family or friends seems to

21. Armstrong, "Why Don't We Talk about How Lonely"; Freiser, "3 Real Feelings You Have"; Kane "Struggles of Working Moms"; MacFadyen, *Don't Mom Alone*; Turner, "Cultivating Deep Friendships."

22. Dellasega, "Hardwired to Care."

miss the mark. Though we also need friendships outside of family, this misconception that family is something separate from friends does not have to be the case. For some, there are family relationships that will never be what we'd like, which we must be realistic about. But maybe they can be better than they currently are. Maybe one relationship with one family member can become a lifeline. Though not many people are talking about it, I believe that prioritizing our extended family is one of the best things we can do for our nuclear family to model the way we can remain connected even as children grow into adults and parents grow into grandparents.

Conclusion

"I've learned that making a 'living' is not the same thing as 'making a life.'"[1]

—Maya Angelou

After finishing reading a book, one might feel inspired and excited to implement things she has taken away from it. Or someone might feel overwhelmed by the amount of information and ideas. If I can leave you with one takeaway, it would be the resolve to keep on. You wouldn't have read this book unless you already cared about being a working homemaker. The way that I do this may be different than the way you do this in a hundred little ways. We need to have the big-picture ideas in place, prioritizing our most precious and limited resource (time with our children) and being willing to do what is best for our family despite its going against contemporary culture and social norms. But beyond this, celebrating our own personality, family culture, and work dynamic are all ways we can glorify God in conduct that is as unique as this world he created. I'm heartened by Sally Clarkson's observation that effective homemakers don't have to fit into a cookie-cutter mold; they just need to share important priorities. She says that the common denominator is "the woman's commitment to make her home consistently welcoming, comfortable, and lifegiving."[2] I am so grateful to be free from the guilt that I must not be a good enough mom because I also choose to work. Knowing ourselves and our giftings, talents, and desires can free us to

1. Quoted in Douglas, *928 Maya Angelou Quotes*, 63.
2. Clarkson, *Mission of Motherhood*, 163.

embrace the lifestyle that allows not just survival but flourishing. I'm also grateful that being an effective worker outside the home doesn't mean I need to aspire to be a "boss babe" and achieve every possible career milestone to prove that I'm a hard worker and a good employee.

One of my favorite stories in the Bible, which is rather underrated in my opinion, is the story of reconciliation between Jacob and Esau. After Jacob had been gone for many years and had grown rich, he traveled back home and met Esau, whom he offered many gifts in an effort to appease him for the grudge he had held. (Remember, Jacob obtained Esau's birthright and blessing.) Although Esau had been angry enough to want to kill Jacob when the ordeal first unfolded, after being offered the gifts, he turned them down, saying, "I already have plenty brother. Keep what you have for yourself" (Genesis 33:9). The truth is, Jacob, who had been greatly blessed by God and who possessed the birthright, likely had more than Esau. We don't really know what happened to Esau during all those years while Jacob was away—the Bible doesn't tell us. But it seems he grew a lot as a person; he learned how to move on, and he found contentment, also having been blessed by God, though maybe not to the same extent as Jacob monetarily. Because we as women have had to work so hard to make a place for ourselves in the workplace and then prove ourselves there, it can be easy to feel the need to vie for our place. There will always be things that make it challenging to be a working woman, especially when we are a working mama. It can be easy to compare ourselves to others, maybe specifically the men we work with, but our experiences are not quite the same and perhaps neither are our goals. Working mamas have been uniquely formed through things like working through morning sickness, finding a bathroom to pump in at a professional event, and being asked yet again how we manage to have both a family and a career. Maybe we are also comparing ourselves with other women, those who don't have children as well as those who do. But the comparison game never fulfills. I haven't experienced the burdens men carry, and everyone's situation is different and challenging, despite the ways we share things in common or differ from other women.

My prayer these days is to realize that, like Esau, I have enough even though I don't have it all. Because it's very likely that Jacob was more successful than Esau, I am especially encouraged by Esau's ability not to become envious of greater worldly success than his but instead to have a vision for his own path. Our vision as working homemakers is to do two things well: to raise our families with love and light and to give back to society through our employment. It's easy to look at those who are successful at work and assume we should follow their lead or even try to compete with them, but they may not have the same home needs or aspirations. Doing our work well without sacrificing the time and energy we need to pour into our families requires selectivity in the sort of work we do as well as an ability to be content with having enough rather than seeking all that might be possible.

For me, recognizing I have plenty also means not romanticizing what my life would be like if I didn't work. Sometimes I idealize homemade food and midday excursions and am tempted to be critical of our home life. Yet, I know I am leaning into my God-given strengths when I help prepare college students to present and defend their ideas. When I compare myself to those who honor God through excellence in domestic arts, what I desire is not really to bake bread but to find the joy that they find when they bake bread. Yet, thankfully, God opted not to make us all carbon copies cut from the same cloth. For me, the joy some find through baking comes instead through writing, helping a student compose an attention grabber at the beginning of his first paragraph, or presenting at a conference. I can't let these academic endeavors keep me from purposefully engaging with my family and creating ample time in my schedule to spend with them, but comparing myself is counterproductive. I'm a professor because I love learning, and others stay home because they love the domestic arts, but neither way in and of itself makes one a good or bad mother. As Justin Whitmel Earley, author of *Habits of the Household*, explains, "Work is not just a way to make the ends of life meet, work is better understood as an end that makes meaning of life."[3] Since we all lead different lives, it makes sense that meaningful work that brings us joy or contentment will vary from person to person. My home has plenty of comfort and homeyness despite our store-bought bread.

We all need to live a life we are convinced of and passionate about. Sometimes I feel a little targeted or get a little offended, if I'm being

---

3. Earley, *Habits of the Household*, 160.

CONCLUSION

honest, when someone posts something on social media about why she knows she is doing the right thing by being a stay-at-home mom. In a similar way, despite the love I have for them, I have felt rather left out chatting with a group of stay-at-home moms as they discussed their ample knowledge of children's book illustrators or sourdough starters. Certain interests and time-intensive activities just don't mesh well with my life. It's easy to interpret the confidence others have in their life choices as a criticism of my doing things differently, but it usually has nothing to do with my situation and my family. It's about their situation and their family. If any of us ever think that our way of doing things is the only way to do them, we'll likely have a rude awakening in our future. We should be leading lives we have prayerfully asked God for wisdom about. If our life does not allow us to spend ample time with our family and intentionally pursue what is worthwhile, we should be open to making a change. But if we are working homemakers with hearts turned toward our children, we need to have enough confidence to be happy for others in their different life choices and situations. First John 3:21 says, "Dear friends, if our hearts do not condemn us, we have confidence before God and receive from him anything we ask, because we keep his commands and do what pleases him." We need to search our hearts and be sure we are not shackled by busyness, accomplishment, or whatever other idols may tempt us. If we can serve our families and our God and our hearts do not condemn us, there is no reason to feel guilt due to someone else's resolve that they are also living a life above reproach.

Intensive mothering[4] is the belief that mothers must provide 24-7 care for their children in order to be good parents. We're not providing intensive parenting, according to the technical definition, as working moms, but things may feel pretty intense just the same. Although we should have ample availability for our children, it's good to acknowledge that despite our commitment to them, we can't be everything for them. It's good to acknowledge the benefit of partnering with others who pour into our children. (Moms who aren't employed must also grapple with this.) Even though we are not with our children 24-7, we are their parents all day every day, and we can be intentional about how to make the

---

4. Hayes, *Cultural Contradictions of Motherhood*.

most of our time with our children. More important than being in our home all day is being purposeful about the hours we do spend there. Ben and I recently went on a trip to New England. It was a dream trip for me, filled with the seaside, history, and literary landmarks. We saw a few museums, but what we spent more time doing was visiting historical homes. There is something powerful about being in the domestic space a person from the past inhabited. Visiting an ornate building is impressive, but seeing where someone committed to daily routines humanizes even the most revered figure. I was able to see the breakfast table where Louisa May Alcott ate with her family. I was able to see the bed that Ralph Waldo Emerson shared with his wife and the robe/overcoat she made him, which he wore over his clothes on chilly mornings. Seeing the homes these literary legends shared with their loved ones reminded me that domestic life is not a sidebar to life—it's what most influences a life. Our homelife does not need to be our entire life, but it should be at the center of it.

The daily rhythms we live out with our husbands and children shape us as people and the things they will then go on to influence. C. S. Lewis said, "The home is the ultimate career. All other careers exist for one purpose, and that is to support the ultimate career."[5] Lewis did not argue for a retreat from the workforce. We can have a career, but it must allow us to cultivate a vibrant homelife rather than inhibit it. If it interferes with our ability to parent our children well, something needs to change. Parenting well doesn't mean making every field trip or being there to put them down for every nap, but it does mean cultivating intentional bonds with our children and husbands. It means protecting our emotional and physical energy reserves. It means committing to little and big moments together, and it means being satisfied with a "smaller" life than we might be able to achieve because thriving is about people, not promotions or public performance. I don't want to make it sound like I have achieved perfect balance with my roles as a mom and a worker. I still sometimes feel insecure when someone reaches a professional milestone I haven't, just like I may feel envious when a mom seems to have mastered a discipline or technique that I haven't. Yet, when I am able to take a posture of gratitude and look at the many

---

5. Original location of statement unknown.

blessings and opportunities God has given me at work and at home, I am able, like Esau, to declare that I have enough. This is my prayer for you as well.

I've said a lot of things. I've unloaded my beliefs about social norms, spiritual formation, home-work balance, and a fair amount in between. I'm humbled to have had your attention, as I know how precious your time is. But I want to leave you with a charge to temper it all with godly wisdom. Something that is often prayed at my church regarding a sermon or teaching that has been given is that God will allow to stand what needs to stand and to fall away what needs to fall away. It has not been my intention to mislead or ill-advise you in any way. But we are all on a life-long journey as parents, and I do not have it all figured out. I am thankful to have learned some things along the way and especially grateful to be given the opportunity to share them.

It will never be easy to be a working mom. Every summer as I head back to work and send my babies back to school, I feel a sadness that still makes me take pause. After ten-plus years, the transition is still hard. In some of the early years, it was so profound that if I had to sign my contract in August rather than the previous May, I may not have signed it. Yet I have learned that some sadness is part of parenting. I felt a sadness when I weaned them, despite the milestone. I will undoubtedly feel sadness when they leave for college (or whatever their next step will be). Yet there has also been and will continue to be so much joy. Raising children means allowing them to experience varying degrees of independence at age-appropriate times. So, if I ever made it sound like being away from them while working is easy, let me clarify: it's often not. There is no worse way to start a Monday morning than dropping off a crying child at daycare and then doing your best to dry your own eyes before walking into the office, even if you know their tears stopped a minute after you left. Yet, at the same time, just as stopping breastfeeding allowed me freedom I didn't know I would enjoy until I regained it, so too does working allow me to use certain giftings and talents that I wouldn't be able to otherwise. Practically speaking, we don't need to feel guilty about enjoying our work. It's possible to both miss our children and take pleasure in an experience away from them.

CONCLUSION

I'm also going to say what may be more disgraceful to admit. Some days going into work is easier: people listen to what we have to say (at least usually), tasks are undertaken and completed, and though we have responsibility, it feels much different than the sort of accountability involved with caring for our children. It may be tempting to pour ourselves out so completely in a job that has quantifiable objectives and outside approval, against which the never-ending cycle of homelife, in which another meal always needs to be cooked and a child always needs guidance, seems to pale in comparison. I admit I have come home irritable at the loudness and mess of our home, not to mention the myriad of tasks awaiting me there. This may happen after a stressful day at work, but it may also happen after experiencing a quiet afternoon in my office grading papers. In these moments of frustration at home when I have not yet switched gears, I have the unrealistic expectation that a private space should function like a public place. Even if I don't take it out on my family, I suffer by not allowing myself the blessing of being present in my homemaking. Being a working homemaker is not just about purposing to be home; it is about cultivating our hearts to love the humble and sanctifying work that happens in our homes. It is also about submitting to the reality that our work is not only what we are paid to do but what we do out of service to our families. Though it honors the Lord to do our work outside the home excellently, we must constantly check our hearts and attitudes to ensure that we can maintain our work performance while also interacting and working well at home and with the other people and places that help enhance our home culture.

So, keep doing the hard work, the good work, and the meaningful work that is both your family and your employment. Galatians 6:9 tells us, "Let us not become weary in doing good, for at the proper time it will reap a harvest if we do not give up." If we are seeking to honor and glorify God through our service to our family and our service to our employer or business (for those who are self-employed), we are doing good. If we are faithful to raise our family, emphasizing faith and relationships, creating margin and healthy boundaries, we will see the fruit of our labor. It won't be immediate, and it may not be constantly, but it will be there. A sweet older brother in Christ whom I work with and attend church with recently told me at a professional development event that he prayed for me on Mother's Day. He also exhorted me that I came to his mind because of the way he had seen my motherhood in action and the peace that he saw in our home. This was kind of shocking because on many a Sunday, I feel frazzled at church, trying to get everyone to sit quietly in the pew, get their snack after the sermon, remember the no-running (or climbing, or throwing) rule at church, and the list goes on. He and I team-taught together one semester, and I also remember some of the hecticness I experienced then, arriving early in the morning, doing all the things required for the family before coming into work. But though my labor wasn't perfect and certainly wasn't always easy, it was still something God was able to take and use. This friend's encouragement that he saw my attempt to do good and the harvest it was reaping in my family's life meant so much to me. Knowing that there are people out there praying for me even when I'm unaware they're doing it is such a comfort. I pray that someone is there to see the good work you are doing and to exhort you and to lift you up to the Father; perhaps you can be that person for someone else. We are all in this together. We are all doing it imperfectly, but God's grace covers that too. As working homemakers, we have the privilege of bringing consistency and intentionality into the spaces we share with our loved ones. May your home and mine be filled with his love and his light.

Bibliography

Abrams, Daniel A., Tianwen Chen, and Vinod Menon. "Neural Circuits Underlying Mother's Voice Perception Predict Social Communication Abilities in Children." *PNAS* 113.22 (2016) 6295–300. https://doi.org/10.1073/pnas.1602948113.

Abrams, Daniel A., Percy K. Mistry, Amanda E. Baker, Aarthi Padmanabhan, and Vinod Menon. "A Neurodevelopmental Shift in Reward Circuity from Mother's to Nonfamilial Voices in Adolescence." *Journal of Neuroscience* 42.20 (2022) 4164–73. https://doi.org/10.1523/JNEUROSCI.2018–21.2022.

Abramson, Ashley. "The Impact of Parental Burnout: What Psychological Research Suggests about How to Recognize and Overcome It." *Monitor On Psychology* 52.7 (October 2021). https://www.apa.org/monitor/2021/10/cover-parental-burnout.

"American and European Workplace Culture Compared." *European Business Review*, September 9, 2021. https://www.europeanbusinessreview.com/american-and-european-workplace-culture-compared-is-the-grass-really-greener/.

Armstrong, Christine. "Why Don't We Talk about How Lonely It Can Be as a Working Mother?" *Grazia*, 2018. https://graziadaily.co.uk/life/real-life/you-re-never-alone-when-you-have-children-but-it-can-be-so-so-lonely/.

Asa, Richard. "Why Cousins Matter: Tapping These Familial Bonds Fosters Insight, Fellowship." *Chicago Tribune*, December 2015. https://www.chicagotribune.com/2015/12/13/why-cousins-matter-tapping-these-familial-bonds-fosters-insight-fellowship/.

Austin, Kyle. "Why Are So Many College Students Rejecting Their Faith?" Collegians for Christ, May 10, 2021. https://www.cfccampusministry.com/why-are-so-many-college-students-rejecting-their-faith.

Baldwin, James. *Giovanni's Room*. New York: Modern Library, 2001.

Battles, Magdalena. *Let Them Play: The Importance of Play and 100 Child Development Activities*. Independently published, 2019.

BBC News. "Children 'Influenced by Parents' Screen-Viewing Habits.'" May 1, 2014. https://www.bbc.com/news/health-27236297.

Behson, Scott. *The Working Dad's Survival Guide: How to Succeed at Work and at Home*. Highlands Ranch, CO: Author's Place, 2015.

Belkin, Lisa. "The Opt-Out Revolution." *New York Times*, October 26, 2003. https://www.nytimes.com/2003/10/26/magazine/the-opt-out-revolution.html.

Billy Graham Evangelistic Association "10 Quote from Billy Graham on Fatherhood." 2024 https://billygraham.org/story/10-quotes-from-billy-graham-on-fatherhood/

BIBLIOGRAPHY

Brady, (Syfers) Judy. "'I Want a Wife,' the Timeless '70s Feminist Manifesto." *The Cut*, from the archives, November 22, 2017. https://www.thecut.com/2017/11/i-want-a-wife-by-judy-brady-syfers-new-york-mag-1971.html.

Brizendine, Louann. *The Female Brain*. New York: Broadway, 2006.

———. *The Male Brain: A Breakthrough Understanding of How Men and Boys Think*. New York: Broadway, 2010.

Brown, Brené. *Daring Greatly: How the Courage to Be Vulnerable Transforms the Way We Live, Love, Parent, and Lead*. New York: Avery, 2012.

Budziszewski, J. *On the Meaning of Sex*. Wilmington, DE: Intercollegiate Studies Institute, 2014.

Bui, Quoctrung, and Claire Cain Miller. "The Typical American Lives Only 18 Miles from Mom." *New York Times*, December 24, 2015. https://www.nytimes.com/interactive/2015/12/24/upshot/24up-family.html.

Calvary Chapel of Jonesboro. "How to Get a Delightful Son—Proverbs 29:17." Proverb a Day. November 26, 2012. https://www.calvarychapeljonesboro.org/proverb-a-day/how-to-get-a-delightful-son-proverbs-2917.

Cambridge Academic Content Dictionary. "Homemaker." 2023. Cited from https://dictionary.cambridge.org/dictionary/english/homemaker.

Chesterton, G. K. *Orthodoxy: With Annotations and Guided Reading by Trevin Wax*. Edited by Trevin Wax. Nashville: B & H Academic, 2022.

Chopin, Kate. *The Awakening*. In *The Awakening and Other Stories*, edited by Pamela Knights, 3–128. Oxford: Oxford University Press, 2008.

Clarkson, Sally. *The Mission of Motherhood: Touching Your Child's Heart of Eternity*. New York: Random House, 2009.

Clarkson, Sally, and Clay Clarkson. *Giving Your Words: The Lifegiving Power of a Verbal Home for Family Faith Formation*. Minneapolis: Bethany House, 2022.

Clarkson, Sally and Sarah Clarkson. *The Lifegiving Home: Creating a Place of Belonging and Becoming*. Carol Stream, IL: Tyndale Momentum, 2016.

Clement, Douglas. "European Vacation: Why Americans Work More than Europeans." Federal Reserve Bank of Minneapolis, December 1, 2003. https://www.minneapolisfed.org/article/2003/european-vacation-why-americans-work-more-than-europeans.

Coleman, Joshua. "A Shift in American Family Values Is Fueling Estrangement" *The Atlantic*, January 2021. https://www.theatlantic.com/family/archive/2021/01/why-parents-and-kids-get-estranged/617612/.

Collins, Patricia Hill. "The Meaning of Motherhood in Black Culture and Black Mother-Daughter Relationships." *Double Stitch: Black Women Write about Mothers and Daughters*, edited by Patricia Bell-Scott, et al, 42–60. Boston: Beacon, 1991.

Cox, Marcelene. *Ladies Home Journal*, 1944.

CVS Health. "The Mental Health Crisis of Working Moms." October 25, 2022. https://www.cvshealth.com/news/mental-health/the-mental-health-crisis-of-working-moms.html.

Dellasega, Cheryl. "Hardwired to Care: The Kin Keepers." In *Forced to Be Family: A Guide to Living with Sinister Sisters, Drama Mamas, and Infuriating In-Laws*, 39–46. Hoboken, NJ: Wiley, 2007.

Diener, E., E. M. Suh, R. E. Lucas, and H. L. Smith. "Subjective Well-Being: Three Decades of Progress." *Psychological Bulletin* 125.2 (1999) 276–302. https://doi.org/10.1037/0033-2909.125.2.276.

Digitale, Erin. "The Teen Brain Tunes in Less to Mom's Voice, More to Unfamiliar Sounds, Study Finds." Stanford Medicine News Center, April 28, 2022. https://med.stanford.edu/news/all-news/2022/04/teenager-brain-mother-voice.html.

DiMickele, Susan. *Chasing Superwoman: A Working Mom's Adventures in Life and Faith*. Colorado Springs: David C. Cook, 2010.

Dobson, James. *Parenting Isn't for Cowards: The 'You Can Do It' Guide for Hassled Parents from America's Best-Loved Family Advocate*. Carol Stream, IL: Tyndale House, 1987.

Doss, B. D., G. K. Rhoades, S. M. Stanley, and H. J. Markman. "The Effect of the Transition to Parenthood on Relationship Quality: An 8-Year Prospective Study." *Journal of Personality and Social Psychology* 96.3 (2009) 601–19. https://doi.org/10.1037/a0013969.

Douglas, Arthur Austen. *928 Maya Angelou Quotes*. India: U B Tech, 2019.

Earley, Justin Whitmel. *Habits of the Household: Practicing the Story of God in Everyday Family Rhythms*. Grand Rapids: Zondervan, 2021.

Elliot, Elisabeth. *The Shaping of a Christian Family: How My Parents Nurtured My Faith*. Grand Rapids: Revell, 1992.

Eliot, T. S. *Notes towards the Definition of Culture*. New York: Harcourt, Brace, 1949.

Emerson, Ralph Waldo. "Self-Reliance." In *The Norton Anthology of American Literature 1820–1865*, edited by Robert S Levine, 236–53. 9th ed. New York: Norton, 2017.

Ennis, Pat, and Lisa Tatlock. "Hospitality Starts with Your Family." Crossway, November 2, 2019. https://www.crossway.org/articles/hospitality-starts-with-your-family/.

Erb, Kelly Phillips. "The Real Cost of Summer Vacation." *Forbes*, July 7, 2014. https://www.forbes.com/sites/kellyphillipserb/2014/07/07/the-real-cost-of-summer-vacation-dont-get-buried-in-taxes/.

Erickson, Jamie. *Holy Hygge: Creating a Place for People to Gather and the Gospel to Grow*. Chicago: Moody, 2022.

"Everyday Heirlooms: Preserving & Teaching Homemaking Skills." Article presented at Brigham Young University Women's Conference, May 1–2, 2008. https://womensconference.byu.edu/sites/womensconference.ce.byu.edu/files/27a_6.pdf.

Feinberg, Mark E., Anna R. Solmeyer, Michelle L. Hostetler, Kari-Lyn Sakuma, Damon Jones, and Susan M McHale. "Siblings Are Special: Initial Test of a New Approach for Preventing Youth Behavior Problems." *Journal of Adolescent Health* 53.2 (2013) 166–73.

Fels, Anna. *Necessary Dreams: Ambition in Women's Changing Lives*. New York: Anchor, 2004.

Fiori, Katherine L., Amy J. Rauer, Kira S. Birditt, Edna Brown, and Terri L. Orbuch. "You Aren't as Close to My Family as You Think: Discordant Perceptions about In-Laws and Risk of Divorce." *Research in Human Development* 17.4 (2020) 258–73. https://doi.org/10.1080/15427609.2021.1874792.

Food Marketing Institute Foundation. "Desires, Barriers and Directions for Shared Meals at Home." 2017. https://www.fmi.org/docs/default-source/familymeals/fmi-power-of-family-meals-whitepaper-for-web.pdf?sfvrsn=13d87f6e_2.

Freiser, Heather. "3 Real Feelings You Have as a Working Parent—and How to Manage Them." *The Muse*, 2022. https://www.themuse.com/advice/feelings-you-experience-working-parent-how-to-manage.

Friedan, Betty. *The Feminine Mystique*. New York: Norton, 2001.

Fry, Richard, Carolina Aragao, Kiley Hurst, and Kim Parker. "In a Growing Share of U.S. Marriages, Husbands and Wives Earn About the Same." Pew Research Center, April

BIBLIOGRAPHY

13, 2023. https://www.pewresearch.org/social-trends/2023/04/13/in-a-growing-share-of-u-s-marriages-husbands-and-wives-earn-about-the-same/.

Garcia, Katelyn M., Corrine N. Carlton, and John A. Richey. "Parenting Characteristics among Adults with Social Anxiety and Their Influence on Social Anxiety Development in Children: A Brief Integrative Review." *Frontier Psychiatry* 12 (2021). https://doi.org/10.3389/fpsyt.2021.614318.

Gardner, Marilyn. "Grandmothers Weigh in on Providing Child Care." *Christian Science Monitor*, August 2002. https://www.csmonitor.com/2002/0814/p16s01-lifp.html.

Gaspard, Terry. "How Parental Relationships Can Improve with Adult Children." The Good Men Project. *Medium*, April 6, 2021. https://medium.com/a-parent-is-born/how-parental-relationships-can-improve-with-adult-children-4d0a9685ca13.

Gates, John. *Destination Truth: Memoirs of a Monster Hunter*. New York: Gallery, 2011.

Gilbertson, Tina. *Reconnecting with Your Estranged Adult Child: Practical Tips and Tools to Heal Your Relationship*. Novato: New World Library, 2020.

Glenn, Norval D., and Charles N. Weaver. "The Contribution of Marital Happiness to Global Happiness." *Journal of Marriage and Family* 43.1 (1981) 161–68. https://doi.org/10.2307/351426.

Global Education Network. "Incredible Benefits of Sharing a Hobby with Your Child." World EDU 2020. https://world.edu/incredible-benefits-of-sharing-a-hobby-with-your-child/.

Goldman, Bruce. "Two Minds: The Cognitive Differences Between Men and Women." *Stanford Medicine Magazine*, May 22, 2017. https://stanmed.stanford.edu/how-mens-and-womens-brains-are-different/.

Gress, Carrie, and Noelle Mering. *Theology of Home II: The Spiritual Art of Homemaking*. Gastonia, NC: Tan, 2020.

Groysberg, Boris, and Robin Abrahams. "Manage Your Work: Manage Your Life." *Harvard Business Review*, March 2014.

Halberstadt, Abbie. *M Is for Mama: A Rebellion against Mediocre Motherhood*. Irvine, CA: Harvest House, 2022.

Haley, Alex. *Roots: The Saga of an American Family*. Boston: D Capo, 2016.

Ham, Ken, Britt Beemer, and Todd Hillard. *Already Gone: Why Your Kids Will Quit Church and What You Can Do to Stop It*. Green Forest, AL: Master, 2009.

Hamaker, Sarah. "The Key Life Skills Parents Should Be Teaching Their Children." *Washington Post*, October 14, 2016. https://www.washingtonpost.com/news/parenting/wp/2016/10/14/the-key-life-skills-parents-should-be-teaching-their-children/.

The Harris Poll. "Are Grandmothers Who Provide Childcare Key in Driving the US Economy?" March 8, 2023. https://theharrispoll.com/briefs/are-grandmothers-who-provide-childcare-key-in-driving-the-us-economy/.

The Hartman Group. "Desires, Barriers and Directions for Shared Meals at Home." Food Marketing Institute Foundation, 2017. https://www.fmi.org/docs/default-source/familymeals/fmi-power-of-family-meals-whitepaper-for-web.pdf.

Hayes, Sharon. *The Cultural Contradictions of Motherhood*. New Haven, CT: Yale University Press, 1996.

Healthline. "Should Toddlers Play Sports? The Answer May Surprise You." 2020. https://www.healthline.com/health/childrens-health/sports-for-toddlers.

Hewlett, Sylvia Ann. "Executive Women and the Myth of Having It All." *Harvard Business Review*, April 2022. https://hbr.org/2002/04/executive-women-and-the-myth-of-having-it-all.

Hochschild, Arlie and Anne Machung. *The Second Shift: Working Families and the Revolution at Home*. New York: Penguin, 2012.

Howe, Nina, and Holly Recchia. "Sibling Relations and Their Impact on Children's Development." In *Encyclopedia on Early Childhood Development*, edited by R. Tremblay, R. Barr, and R. Peters, 1–8. Quebec: Centre of Excellence for Early Childhood Development, 2006.

Hunt, Leigh. *The Indicator*. No. 49. 1821.

"Infant Baptism." *Catholic Answers*, 2023. https://www.catholic.com/tract/infant-baptism.

Italie, Leanne. "Working Families Enlist Grandparents to Help with the Kids." *PBS News Hour*, 2020. https://www.pbs.org/newshour/nation/working-families-enlist-grandparents-to-help-with-the-kids.

Jimenez Law Firm. "Why Women Initiate Divorce More Often than Men." 2022. https://www.thejimenezlawfirm.com/why-women-initiate-divorce-more-often-than-men/.

Johnson, Jamie. "The Average Cost of a Vacation." *Lend EDU*, January 19, 2022. https://lendedu.com/blog/average-vacation-cost/#expenses.

Kane, Maria. "The Struggles of Working Moms: Battling Loneliness, Overwhelm, and Exhaustion" Linked In, 2023. HYPERLINK "https://www.linkedin.com/pulse/struggles-working-moms-battling-loneliness-overwhelm-exhaustion-kane/"(22) The Struggles of Working Moms: Battling Loneliness, Overwhelm, and Exhaustion | LinkedIn

Kelley, Susan. "Want More Sex? Split the Household Chores." *Cornell Chronicle*, August 2, 2016. https://news.cornell.edu/stories/2016/08/want-more-sex-split-household-chores.

Kingson, Jennifer A. "Women in the Law Say Path is Limited by 'Mommy Track.'" *The New York Times*, 1988. https://www.nytimes.com/1988/08/08/us/women-in-the-law-say-path-is-limited-by-mommy-track.html

Kirchheimer, Sid. "Overscheduled Child May Lead to a Bored Teen." *WebMD*, 2004. https://www.webmd.com/parenting/features/overscheduled-child-may-lead-to-bored-teen.

Lindsey, Linda Lee. *Gender Roles: A Sociological Perspective*. New York: Routledge, 2014.

Liu, Shijing, Wadeson, Amy, Kim, Na Young, & Nam, Chang S. (2016). "Effects of Working Memory Capacity, Task Switching, and Task Difficulty on Multitasking Performance." *Proceedings of the Human Factors and Ergonomics Society Annual Meeting*, 60(1), 502–506. https://doi.org/10.1177/1541931213601114

Loden, Marilyn. Panel discussion at the Women's Action Alliance. 1978.

Lythcott-Haims, Julie. *How to Raise an Adult: Break Free of the Overparenting Trap and Prepare Your Kid for Success*. New York: St. Martin's, 2015.

MacFadyen, Heather. *Don't Mom Alone: Growing the Relationships You Need to Be the Mom You Want to Be*. Grand Rapids: Baker, 2021.

Mackenzie, Sarah. *The Read-Aloud Family: Making Meaningful and Lasting Connections with Your Kids*. Grand Rapids: Zondervan, 2018.

Mailey, Emily L., and Edward McAuley. "Impact of a Brief Intervention on Physical Activity and Social Cognitive Determinants among Working Mothers: A Randomized Trial." *Journal of Behavioral Medicine* 37 (2014) 343–55. https://doi.org/10.1007/s10865-013-9492-y.

BIBLIOGRAPHY

Martin, William. *The Parent's Tao Te Ching: Ancient Advice for Modern Parents.* Philadelphia: Da Capo Lifelong, 1999.

Mason, Mary Ann, Nicholas H. Wolfinger, and Marc Goulden. *Do Babies Matter?: Gender and Family in the Ivory Tower.* New Brunswick: Rutgers University, 2013.

Matchar, Emily. *Homeward Bound: Why Women Are Embracing the New Domesticity.* New York: Simon and Schuster, 2015.

Maushart, Susan. *The Mask of Motherhood: How Becoming a Mother Changes Our Lives and Why We Never Talk about It.* New York: Penguin, 2000.

Mayol-García, Yerís. "Children Continue to Be More Involved with Extracurricular Activities." United States Census Bureau, July 2022. https://www.census.gov/library/stories/2022/07/children-continue-to-be-involved-in-extracurricular-activities.html.

McGee, David, and Bryce Hantla. "The Portrayal of Fathers in Popular Media." *Journal of Discipleship and Family Ministry* 3.2 (2013) 36–46. https://digitalcommons.liberty.edu/sod_fac_pubs/57/.

McKay, David O. *Family Home Evening Manual 1968–69.* Council of the Twelve Apostles, 1968.

McKendrick, Joe. "Another Benefit of Hybrid Work: A Shift from Hustle Culture to Outcome Culture." *Forbes*, March 23, 2023. https://www.forbes.com/sites/joemckendrick/2023/03/23/another-benefit-of-hybrid-work-a-shift-from-hustle-culture-to-outcome-culture/.

Mead, Margaret. *Blackberry Winter: My Early Years.* New York: Kodansha, 1995.

Melser, Nancy Armstrong. *Soft Skills for Kids: In Schools, at Home, and Online.* 2nd ed. Lanham, MD: Rowman & Littlefield, 2022.

Mental Health Foundation. "Men and Women: Statistics." 2023. https://www.mentalhealth.org.uk/explore-mental-health/statistics/men-women-statistics.

Merriam-Webster.com Dictionary. "Home away from home." https://www.merriam-webster.com/dictionary/home%20away%20from%20home.

Milardo, Robert M. *The Forgotten Kin: Aunts and Uncles.* Cambridge: Cambridge University, 2010.

Miller, Arthur. *Death of a Salesman.* In *The Norton Anthology of American Literature. Volume E: Literature Since 1945 Ninth ed*, edited by Robert S Levin, 221–286. New York: Norton, 2017.

Montgomery, Lucy Maud. *Anne of Green Gables.* New York: Sterling, 2004.

Moore, Thomas. *Care of the Soul: How to Add Depth and Meaning to Your Everyday Life.* New York: Harper Collins, 1992.

Morin, Amy. "How to Create Stronger Bonds among Siblings." *Very Well Family*, August 2021. https://www.verywellfamily.com/how-to-create-stronger-bonds-among-siblings-4778201.

Nelson, Audrey. "Differences in Nonverbal Cues between Men and Women." *Psychology Today*, March 15, 2022. https://www.psychologytoday.com/us/blog/he-speaks-she-speaks/202203/differences-in-nonverbal-cues-between-men-and-women.

Nelson, Julie K. "Sharing Hobbies with Your Child." *Family Today*, 2021. https://www.familytoday.com/family/sharing-hobbies-with-your-child/.

Nobel, Carmen. "Kids Benefit from Having a Working Mom." *Harvard Business School*, May 15, 2015. https://hbswk.hbs.edu/item/kids-benefit-from-having-a-working-mom.

O'Connor, Flannery. "Good Country People." In *The Norton Anthology of American Literature. Volume E: Literature Since 1945 Ninth ed*, edited by Robert S Levin, 435–449. New York: Norton, 2017.

BIBLIOGRAPHY

Oppenheimer, Lisa. "The Real Reason Moms Need Vacations." *HuffPost*, February 1, 2014. https://www.huffpost.com/entry/the-real-reason-moms-need-vacations_b_4602864.

Otto, Luther B., Maxine P. Atkinson, Karyl E. MacEwen, and Julian Barling. "Maternal Employment Experiences and Children's Behavior: A Reanalysis and Comment." *Journal of Marriage and Family* 56.2 (1994) 501–10. https://doi.org/10.2307/353116.

Patterson, Dorothy. *Handbook for Ministers' Wives*. Nashville: Broadman & Holman, 2002.

Pelley, Virginia. "The Profound Importance of Having 'Couple Friends.'" *Fatherly*, updated October 26, 2021. https://www.fatherly.com/love-money/the-profound-importance-of-having-couples-friends.

Perry, Mark J. "There Really Is No 'Gender Wage Gap.' There's a 'Gender Earnings Gap' but 'Paying Women Well' Won't Close That Gap." American Enterprise Institute, July 31, 2017. https://www.aei.org/carpe-diem/there-really-is-no-gender-wage-gap-there-is-a-gender-earnings-gap-but-paying-women-well-wont-close-that-gap/.

Pew Research Center. "Parenting in America." December 17, 2015. https://www.pewresearch.org/social-trends/2015/12/17/parenting-in-america/.

Pieper, Kevin. "The Beauty Concept." In *Connecting with Nature: Portraits and Essays on Nature and Man*. Battle Ground, WA: Pediment, 2010.

Pope Pius XII. "Allocution to the Fathers of Families." Available at https://www.ewtn.com/catholicism/library/allocution-to-the-fathers-of-families-8939.

Ram, Natalie. "DNA by the Entirety." *Columbia Law Review*. 115 (2015): 873–938.

Renner, Ben. "Fathers Today More Engaged with Their Kids 'Than Ever Before,' Study Finds." *Study Finds*, 2022. https://studyfinds.org/fathers-more-engaged-with-kids-than-ever-before/

Ribar, David C. "Why Marriage Matters for Child Wellbeing." *The Future of Children* 25.2 (2015): 11–27. http://www.jstor.org/stable/43581970.

Rich, Adrienne. *Of Woman Born: Motherhood as Experience and Institution*. New York: Norton, 1995.

Ringstaff, Melissa. "Demonstrating the Gospel: Why the Gospel Is Important." *A Virtuous Woman*, 2023. https://avirtuouswoman.org/homemaking-important/.

Rinker, Dirk, and Michael Jaffarian. "15 Million Americans Have Left Christianity in the Past Ten Years." ACS Technologies, 2022. https://www.acstechnologies.com/church-growth/15-million-americans-have-left-christianity-in-the-past-ten-years/.

Robb, Michael. "Why Watching TV and Movies Is Better Together: Co-Viewing Tips to Promote Learning and Bonding." *Common Sense Media*, December 2021. https://www.commonsensemedia.org/articles/why-watching-tv-and-movies-is-better-together.

Robinson, Marilynne. *Lila*. New York: Farrar, Straus and Giroux, 2014.

Rosenfeld, Alvin, and Nicole Wise. *Hyper-Parenting: Are You Hurting Your Child by Trying Too Hard?* New York: St. Martin's, 2011.

Rubin, Gretchen. "Agree, Disagree? Home Is a Physical Space; It's Also a State of Mind." October 23, 2015. https://gretchenrubin.com/articles/agree-disagree-home-is-a-physical-space-its-also-a-state-of-mind/.

Savage, Jill. *Professionalizing Motherhood: Encouraging, Educating, and Equipping Mothers at Home*. Grand Rapids: Zondervan, 2002.

Schulze, K. A., S. Rule, and M. S. Innocenti. Coincidental Teaching: Parents Promoting Social Skills at Home. *Teaching Exceptional Children* 21.2 (1989) 24–27. https://doi.org/10.1177/004005998902100205.

BIBLIOGRAPHY

Seltzer, Rick. "Gender Roles and Presidential Spouses." *Inside Higher Ed*, January 9, 2017. https://www.insidehighered.com/news/2017/01/10/survey-finds-gender-gap-presidential-spouse-expectations.

Semeco, Arlene. "What Happens if You Drink Too Much Water?" *Medical News Today*. December 19, 2023. https://www.medicalnewstoday.com/articles/318619

Sharma, M.D. *Top Inspiring Thoughts of Benjamin Franklin*. N.p.: Prabhat Prakashan, 2015.

"Shorter Catechism of the Assembly of Divines" (Westminster Shorter Catechism). July 28, 1648. Availalbe at https://www.apuritansmind.com/westminster-standards/shorter-catechism/.

Silberman, Charles. *Crisis in the Classroom: The Remaking of American Education*. New York: Random House, 1970.

Spurgeon, Charles. "Christ's People - Imitators of Him" New Park Street Pulpit Volume 1. April 29, 1855. https://www.spurgeon.org/resource-library/sermons/christs-people-imitators-of-him/

Stackhouse, John G., Jr. *Partners in Christ: A Conservative Case for Egalitarianism*. Downers Grove, IL: IVP Academic, 2015.

Suttie, Jill. "How Your Siblings Can Make You Happier." *Greater Good Magazine*, May 27, 2022. https://greatergood.berkeley.edu/article/item/how_your_siblings_can_make_you_happier.

Szczygiel, Veronica. "How to Foster a Faith-Filled Home When Your Spouse Isn't Full of Faith." *Busted Halo*, May 31, 2023. https://bustedhalo.com/life-culture/how-to-foster-a-faith-filled-home-when-your-spouse-isnt-full-of-faith.

Tartakovsky, Margarita. "This Is How You Can Cope with Being a Working Mom." *PsychCentral*, January 2022.

Teresa of Avila. *The Interior Castle*. Translated by Kieran Kavanaugh. Study ed. 2nd ed., rev. Washington, DC: Institute of Carmelite Studies Pub., 2020.

Theology of Work Project. "God Creates and Equips People to Work." https://www.theologyofwork.org/old-testament/genesis-1-11-and-work/god-creates-and-equips-people-to-work-genesis-126-225//#fruitfulness-growth-genesis-128-215-19-20.

"The Role of Music in Brain Development." University of Georgia Extension. December 2022. https://secure.caes.uga.edu/extension/publications/files/pdf/C%201053-06_5.PDF

Thompson, Stephanie. "Families Only Spend 37 Minutes Together a Day: Make Them Count." *Parent Cue*, 2021. https://theparentcue.org/families-only-spend-37-minutes-together-a-day-make-them-count/.

Thoreau, Henry David. "'Early Spring in Massachusetts' from the Journal of Henry David Thoreau" edited by H. G. O. Blake in *The Writings of Henry David Thoreau with Bibliographical Introductions and Full Indexes V 5*. Boston: Houghton Mifflin Company, 1883.

Tsang, Anna. "The Effects of Working Mothers on Sibling Rivalry." *Undergraduate Research Journal for the Human Sciences* 8 (2009). https://publications.kon.org/urc/v8/tsang.html.

Turner, Jessica N. "Cultivating Deep Friendships." In *Stretched Too Thin: How Working Moms Can Lose the Guilt, Work Smarter, and Thrive*, 187–206. Grand Rapids: Revell, 2018.

"U.S. Families Spend the Most Time Together on Vacation." *Lodging Magazine*, March 29, 2018. https://lodgingmagazine.com/american-families-spend-most-time-together-vacation/.

"Visit Anaheim Study Reveals American Families Spend the Most Quality Time Together While on Vacation." Visit Aneheim, March 1, 2018. https://www.visitanaheim.org/articles/post/visit-anaheim-study-reveals-american-families-spend-the-most-quality-time-together-while-on-vacation/.

Waitt, G., and Patricia Macquarie. "Travel-as-Homemaking." In *Travel and Imagination*, edited by G. Lean, R. Staiff, and E. Waterton, 53–71. Farnham, UK: Ashgate, 2014.

Weir, Kristen. "Improving Sibling Relationships." *Monitor on Psychology* 53.2 (March 1, 2022). https://www.apa.org/monitor/2022/03/feature-sibling-relationships.

Weis, Fern. "The Real Reason Your Kids Act Worse for You than Anyone Else—and How to Help." *Motherly*, December 1, 2017. https://www.mother.ly/parenting/the-real-reason-your-kids-act-worse-for-you-than-anyone-elseand-how-to-help/.

Why Multitasking Doesn't Work." Cleveland Clinic. March 10, 2021. https://health.clevelandclinic.org/science-clear-multitasking-doesnt-work

Williams, Joan. *Unbending Gender: Why Family and Work Conflict and What to Do about It*. Oxford: Oxford University, 2001.

Wilson, Andrew. "The Key to Saving Teenagers." *Think Theology*, June 8, 2015. https://thinktheology.co.uk/blog/article/the_key_to_saving_teenagers.

Wirthlin, Joseph B. "Spiritually Strong Homes and Families." *Ensign*, May 1993, 68–72.

Wood, Donald. "Americans Prioritizing Travel—Using More Vacation Days." *Travel Pulse*, July 20, 2022. https://www.travelpulse.com/news/impacting-travel/americans-prioritizing-travel-using-more-vacation-days.html.

Wunder, Wendy. *The Probability of Miracles*. New York: Razorbill, 2012.

Yavorsky, Jill E., Lisa A. Keister, Yue Qian, and Sarah Thébaud. "Separate Spheres: The Gender Division of Labor in the Financial Elite." *Social Forces* 102.2 (2023): 609–32. https://doi.org/10.1093/sf/soado61.

Yorgason, Jeremy B., and Kathryn B. Gustafson. "Linking Grandparent Involvement with the Development of Prosocial Behavior in Adolescents." In *Prosocial Development: A Multidimensional Approach*, edited by Laura M Padilla-Walker and Gustavo Walker, 201–20. Oxford: Oxford University, 2014.

Zucker, Rebecca. "Breaking Free from a '9 to 5' Culture." *Harvard Business Review*, July 27, 2021. https://hbr.org/2021/07/breaking-free-from-a-9-to-5-culture.

www.ingramcontent.com/pod-product-compliance
Lightning Source LLC
Chambersburg PA
CBHW071428160426
43195CB00013B/1844